Science Olympiad

Highly useful for all school students participating
in Various Olympiads & Competitions

Series Editor Keshav Mohan

Authors

Preeti Gupta (Chemistry) • *Karuna Thakur* (Physics) • *Shikha* (Biology)

Class
6

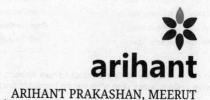

arihant

ARIHANT PRAKASHAN, MEERUT

ARIHANT PRAKASHAN, MEERUT

All Rights Reserved

ॐ **Administrative & Production Offices**

Corporate Office   'Ramchhaya' 4577/15, Agarwal Road, Darya Ganj New Delhi -110002
Tele: 011- 47630600, 43518550; Fax: 011- 23280316

Head Office   Kalindi, TP Nagar, Meerut (UP) - 250002
Tele: 0121-2401479, 2512970, 4004199; Fax: 0121-2401648

All disputes subject to Meerut (UP) jurisdiction only.

ॐ **Sales & Support Offices**

Agra, Ahmedabad, Bengaluru, Bhubaneswar, Bareilly, Chennai, Delhi, Guwahati, Haldwani, Hyderabad, Jaipur, Jalandhar, Jhansi, Kolkata, Kota, Lucknow, Meerut, Nagpur & Pune

ॐ **ISBN**   978-93-5203-402-4

ॐ **Price**   ₹95

Typeset by Arihant DTP Unit at Meerut
Printed & Bound by Arihant Publications (I) Ltd. (Press Unit)

Production Team

Publishing Manager	Mahendra Singh Rawat	Cover Designer	Syed Darin Zaidi
Project Head	Karishma Yadav	Inner Designer	Deepak Kumar
Project Coordinator	Divya Gusain	Page Layouting	Divakar Gaur
Proof Reader	Mehtab Alam	DTP Operator	Ashwani

For further information about the products from Arihant
log on to www.arihantbooks.com or email to info@arihantbooks.com

Preface

Science Olympiad Series for Class 6th -10th is a series of books which will challenge the young inquisitive minds by the non-routine and exciting problems based on concept of Science.

The main purpose of this series is to make the students ready for competitive exams. The school/board exams are of qualifying nature but not competitive, they do not help the students to prepare for competitive exams, which mainly have objective questions.

- **Need of Olympiad Series**
  This series will fill this gap between the School/Board and Competitive Exams as this series have all questions in Objective format. This series helps students who are willing to sharpen their problem solving skills. Unlike typical assessment books, which emphasis on drilling practice, the focus of this series is on practicing problem solving techniques.

- **Development of Logical Approach**
  The thought provoking questions given in this series will help students to attain a deeper understanding of the concepts and through which students will be able to impart reasoning/Logical/Analytical skills in them.

- **Complement Your School Studies**
  This series complements the additional preparation needs of students for regular school/board exams. Along with, it will also address all the requirements of the students who are approaching National/State level competitions or Olympiads.

We shall welcome criticism from the students, teachers, educators and parents. We shall also like to hear from all of you about errors and deficiencies, which may have remained in this edition and the suggestions for the next edition.

Editors & Authors

Contents

OLYMPIAD Class 6

Chapter 1

Food: Where does It Come From?

A Introduction

1. Female mosquitoes live on blood that they suck from humans and other animals. They have a long, sharp pipe-like structure instead of teeth, that is used to pierce the skin and suck blood. Male mosquitoes on the contrary feeds on plant sap and nectar. Identify the category to which they belong?

	Female	Male
a	Herbivorous	Omnivorous
b	Herbivorous	Herbivorous
c	Sanguivorous	Herbivorous
d	Carnivorous	Carnivorous

2. Green plants are known as producers or autotrophs. They prepare more food than they require. The extra food is stored in different parts of the plant. Observe the parts of the plant from which the following eatables (*P*, *Q*, *R* and *S*) and select the correct option.

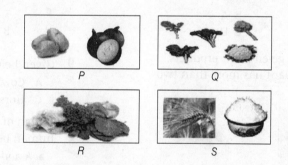

P

Q

R

S

Codes

	P	Q	R	S
a	Stem	Leaf	Flower	Seed
b	Root	Flower	Leaf	Fruit
c	Stem	Flower	Leaf	Seed
d	Root	Flower	Leaf	Seed

3. The figures given below show "This eats that." Find who is prey?

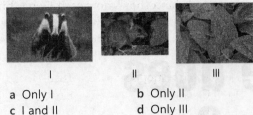

I	II	III

  a Only I   b Only II
  c I and II   d Only III

4. In the given short segments of food chain, which ones are incorrect with respect to the correct order food chain?

   I. Lion – Goat   II. Lizard – Rat
  III. Snake – Rat   IV. Goat – Grain
   V. Insect – Spider   VI. Lizard – Spider

Codes
  a II, III and VI   b II, III, V and VI
  c II, V and VI   d II and V

5. Observe the figure given below and among the labelled parts, which one is not used as food?

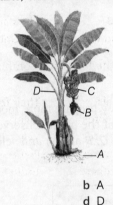

  a B   b A
  c C   d D

6. From the below given plant products. Whose parent plant has more than two edible parts?

  a A and B
  b B and C
  c C and D
  d A and D

7. Match the column I with column II.

	Column I		Column II
A.	Cabbage	1.	Root
B.	Carrot	2.	Seed
C.	Peas	3.	Fruit
D.	Apple	4.	Leaf
E.	Cauliflower	5.	Flower

Codes

	A	B	C	D	E
a	4	1	2	3	5
b	3	1	2	4	5
c	4	2	1	3	5
d	4	5	2	3	1

8. In the flow chart given below, the organisms are categorised on the basis of their food requirements. Identify *A*, *B* and *C*.

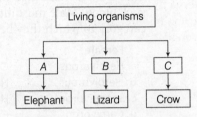

Codes

	Autotrophs	Herbivores	Carnivores	Omnivores
a	A	B	C	–
b	–	A	B	C
c	–	B	A	C
d	B	C	A	–

9. Given below are names of some animals.
  A. Cow   B. Sheep
  C. Horse   D. Ox

Which of the above are sources of milk for human beings?
  a A and C
  b A and B
  c A and D
  d Only A

10. Study each of the given set carefully. Identify the odd one.
  a Cow, milk, butter
  b Hen, egg, meat
  c Goat, milk, meat
  d Plant, vegetable, butter, milk

11. In the given below two groups different types of eatables and their varieties are given. Opt the option that correctly declares the eatables with the variety to which they belong.

Group I

A. Chana and Mung   B. Brinjal and Carrot

C. Pepper and Chilly   D. Kiwi

E. Broccoli and Cabbage

Group II

P. Vegetables   Q. Spices

R. Pulses   S. Salad

T. Fruit

Codes

	A	B	C	D	E
a	R	T	Q	S	P
b	Q	P	R	S	T
c	R	P	S	R	T
d	R	P	Q	T	S

12. Observe the given below options considering their food habits, which of the following is a scavenger?

a

b

c

d

13. Observe the figure given below and find out from which part of the plant, is it obtained from?

a Stem   b Seeds

c Leaves   d Fruits

14.

I	II	III	IV
Cinchona	Isabgol	Neem	*Rauwolfia*

Which of the above labelled names are designated correctly by given options?

a I, III are medicinal plants and II, IV are the products of medicinal plants.

b II, III are medicinal plants and I, IV are spices.

c I, II, IV are medicinal products not plants and III is a medicinal plant.

d I, II, III and IV all are medicinal plants.

15. There are some components of food chain given below. Each of them has a labelling. A food chain shows how each living things get its food. It shows 'who is eating whom'. Now, you have to figure out 'hawk' eats 'whom'.

A. Grasshopper   B. Toad

C. Grass   D. Parrot

E. Snake   F. Nettle

G. Bird   H. Lion

Codes

a F   b E

c B   d H

16. Which of the following is correct?

	Plant product	Animal product	Omnivore
A	Bamboo	Crab	Camel
B	Brinjal	Asparagus	Rabbit
C	Honey	Milk	Horse
D	Grains	Eggs	Man

a A and B   b B and C

c A, B and C   d Only D

17. Which of the following combination(s) is/are correct?

Animals	Their food
A. Carnivores	Meat
B. Herbivores	Vegetables
C. Omnivores	Plants
D. Scavengers	Fruits

Codes

a A and B   b B and C

c C and D   d All except D

18. Consider the given statements and opt the option that correctly declares them either true or false.

I. Eggs are a rich source of meat.

II. Flesh of animals is known as meat.

III. Aquaculture includes rearing of fish, crabs, lobsters, etc.

IV. Poultry farm is the place used to rear birds.

V. Almond is a dry nut.

Codes

	I	II	III	IV	V
a	T	T	T	T	T
b	T	T	T	T	F
c	F	T	T	T	T
d	F	F	F	F	F

19. Which of the following statements is/are incorrect?

    A. Animals consume the food prepared and stored by green plants.

    B. Dandelion is used as a type of food.

    C. Camel is a herbivorous animal.

    D. Plants depend on animals for their food.

    E. Sprouts contain more of fats, which makes them nutritious.

Choose the correct option.

    a A and B
    b C and D
    c D and E
    d A, C and E

20. Consider the passage given below and opt the option that correctly fills the missing blanks.

Animals like cows, buffaloes and __A__ provide us milk. Milk is rich in proteins, __B__, carbohydrates, vitamins and minerals. The animals that produce milk are __C__. Like milk, honey is also obtained from animals. It is very nutritious in nature. Honeybees collect nectar from different flowers, mix it with a secretion from their __D__ and convert it into honey.

Codes

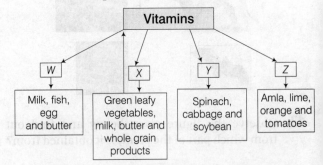

	A	B	C	D
a	sheeps	fat	producers	beehives
b	goats	dietery fibres	carnivores	petals
c	sheeps	dietery fibres	omnivores	pollen grains
d	goats	fat	herbivores	mouth

B   Components of Food

1. Riya is a school going teenager. She takes healthy diet but fibre rich food is missing in it. Select one of the following food items that she needs.

a

b

c

d

2. In the figure given below, the white thread-like structures emerging from grains are rich in which of the following components?

    A. Proteins   B. Vitamins

    C. Carbohydrates   D. Minerals

Codes

    a A and B
    b B and C
    c C and D
    d A, B, C and D

3. In the flow chart given below, what would you write at the places of W, X, Y and Z?

```
                    Vitamins
       ┌──────────┬──────────┬──────────┐
      W           X           Y           Z
      │           │           │           │
  Milk, fish,   Green leafy  Spinach,   Amla, lime,
  egg          vegetables,  cabbage and orange and
  and butter   milk, butter and soybean tomatoes
               whole grain
               products
```

Note A, B, C, D, E, K in the options are vitamins

Codes

	W	X	Y	Z		W	X	Y	Z
a	A	B	D	C	b	D	E	K	C
c	E	D	K	C	d	A	D	K	C

4. Consider the statements given below and identify which component is being talked about?

    I. It is required for making bones and teeths.

    II. It helps in blood clotting.

    III. It helps in proper working of muscles.

    IV. It is obtained from milk, cheese, green vegetables, etc.

Codes

    a Iron   b Calcium
    c Iodine   d Phosphorus

5. Complete the table by opting the correct option.

Vitamin/ Mineral	Deficiency disease	Symptom
Vitamin-A	A	B
Vitamin-B$_1$	C	D
Vitamin-C	Scurvy	Bleeding gums

Codes

	A	B	C	D
a	Beri-beri	Poor vision	Night blindness	Loss of vision in darkness
b	Night blindness	Poor vision in darkness	Beri beri	Weak muscles
c	Rickets	Weak muscles	Night blindness	Loss of vision in darkness
d	Anaemia	Blood loss	Beri-beri	Weak muscles

6. Some minerals and their deficiency diseases are given below. Select the incorrect match.

- A. Iron   –   Anaemia
- B. Calcium   –   Rickets
- C. Iodine   –   Goitre
- D. Phosphorus –   Marasmus
- E. Fluorine   –   Muscle cramps
- F. Manganese –   Osteoporosis

Codes
- a A, B and C
- b C, E and F
- c B, D and F
- d D and E

7. Match the column I with column II.

	Column I		Column II
A.	Carbohydrates	1.	Growth and repair
B.	Fats	2.	Normal functioning of body
C.	Proteins	3.	Provide energy
D.	Vitamins	4.	Maintain good health
E.	Minerals	5.	Act as insulator for body

Codes

	A	B	C	D	E
a	5	3	1	4	2
b	3	5	1	2	4
c	1	5	3	4	2
d	2	4	1	3	5

8. Which of the following is the correct categorisation of water and fat soluble vitamins?

	Water soluble vitamins	Fat soluble vitamins
a	C, D, K	A, B
b	A, B	C, D, E, K
c	A, D, K, E	B, C
d	B, C	A, D, E, K

9. Choose the correct option with respect to dietary fibres.

	Energy	Vitamins	Digestion	Blood formation
a	✓	✓	✗	✓
b	✓	✗	✓	✓
c	✗	✗	✓	✗
d	✓	✓	✓	✗

10. Which of the following is/are correct tests for food nutrients?

	Test	Observation	Result
1.	Potato + Dil. iodine	Blue-black colour	Starch present
2.	Soybean + Dil. NaOH + Cu$_2$SO$_4$	Voilet colour	Protein absent
3.	Flour + Dil. iodine	Yellow colour	Eat present
4.	Egg white + Dil. iodine	No blue-black colour	Starch absent

Codes
- a 1 and 2   b 2 and 3   c 3 and 4   d 4 and 1

11. Groundnuts are one of the nutritious food. It is more nutritious than wheat. In its composition, it contains

- A. protein   B. vitamin
- C. fat   D. carbohydrate

Codes
- a A and B   b A, C and D
- c C and D   d A, B, C and D

12. Manish was having difficulty in seeing things in dim light. The doctor tested his eyesight and prescribed a particular vitamin supplement. He also advised him to include a few food items like carrot, papaya, mango, milk and fish oil in his diet.

Which component Manish lacks and from which disease he is suffering?

- a Vitamin-D – Rickets
- b Vitamin-A – Night blindness
- c Vitamin-B – Night blindness
- d Vitamin-B$_1$ – Beri-beri

13. Observe the given figures *P* and *Q* carefully.

Figure *P* shows a normal artery (type of blood vessel) and figure *Q* shows a disturbed condition of artery in which it has became narrow.

Narrowing of the artery in the figure *Q* may be due to

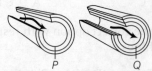

    a deposition of proteins
    b deposition of carbohydrates
    c deposition of vitamin-D
    d deposition of fats

14. Which of the following statements are correct?
    A. Minerals and vitamins are needed in large quantities, as they are not retained by our body for long time.
    B. Minerals and vitamins protect our body against diseases.
    C. Minerals and vitamins promote growth.
    D. Mineral and vitamins help us in maintaining good health.

Choose the correct option.
    a A and B   b B and C
    c C and D   d Both b and c

15. Carefully observe the steps given below and answer the question that follows.
    Step I   Take a small amount of soybean seeds.
    Step II Wrap the food items in a small piece of paper.
    Step III Crush the seeds in that paper.
    Step IV Take out the crushed seed from the paper.

From the options below, which one you will use after step IV to test the presence of fat by observing under sunlight?
    a Seeds
    b Paper
    c May be seed or paper
    d Seeds and paper are compulsory to test the presence of fat.

16. Carbohydrates are of great importance. They are usually sweet in nature except some. They are easily found in our food in the form of sugar, starch, cellulose, etc. From the options, given below opt the correct combinations of carbohydrate and its source.

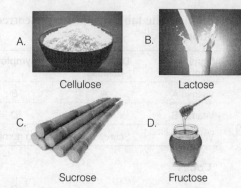

A.   B.
Cellulose   Lactose

C.   D.
Sucrose   Fructose

Codes
    a A and B
    b B and C
    c B, C and D
    d D and A

17. Two figures *X* and *Y* given below. Opt the option that declares their correct properties

X   *Y*

    a *X* is the simple carbohydrate having sweet taste and *Y* is the complex carbohydrate, which is tasteless in nature.
    b *Y* is the simple carbohydrate having sweet taste and *X* is the complex carbohydrate, which is tasteless in nature.
    c *X* is the simple carbohydrate but tasteless and *Y* is the complex carbohydrate with sweet taste.
    d None of the above

18. Observe the figure below and fill the blanks accordingly.

A. Food item rich in carbohydrates is __(i)__ .
B. Egg is rich source of protein, the mineral __(ii)__ and vitamin __(iii)__ .
C. __(iv)__ is a rich source of fat.
D. Milk provides __(v)__ , vitamin-D and __(iv)__ (mineral).

Codes

	(i)	(ii)	(iii)	(iv)	(v)	(vi)
a	spinach	calcium	D	Spinach	protein	Mg
b	chapatti	calcium	D	Butter	protein	Ca
c	papaya	iodine	K	Egg	protein	P
d	orange	iodine	K	Butter	protein	K

19. Consider the given statement and opt the option that correctly states them either true(T) or false(F).

   I. Roughage helps in maintaining the digestive system healthy.

   II. Iodine helps in making blood.

   III. Vitamin-A can be prepared by our body in the presence of sunlight.

   IV. Sodium and potassium helps in maintaining fluid balance in body.

   V. Anaemia is a disease caused by the deficiency of iodine.

   ### Codes

	I	II	III	IV	V
a	T	T	T	T	T
b	T	F	F	T	F
c	F	T	F	T	F
d	T	T	T	F	T

20. **Assertion** (A) Water does not provide nutrients, yet it is an important component of food.

   Reason (R) It helps to absorb nutrients from food.

   a Both A and R are true and R is the correct explanation of A.

   b Both A and R are true, but R is not the correct explanation of A.

   c A is true, but R is false.

   d Both A and R are false.

21. The chart shows differences between some fruits.

   Which fruit is most probably low in fat and high in fibre and vitamin-C ?

   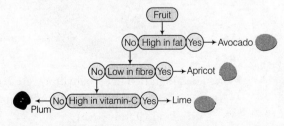

   a Avocado   b Apricot
   c Plum   d Lime

Direction (Q.No. 22)

Observe the graph given below and answer the question that follows:

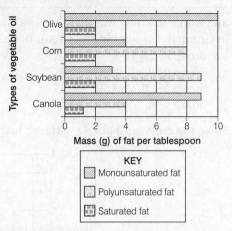

22. Which of the above type of vegetable oil is good for our health?

   a Corn

   b Soybean

   c Olive

   d Canola

23. The table below shows sources, functions and deficiency diseases caused by some vitamins and minerals.

Vitamin/Mineral	Source	Function
Vitamin-C	Oranges, lemons and grapes	Makes skin and gums healthy and heal wounds quickly
Vitamin-D	Milk, butter, eggs, fish and liver	Makes bones and teeth strong
Calcium	Milk and eggs	Makes bones and teeth strong
Phosphorus	Milk, apple, beans, dry fruits and pulses	Helps in the body development and makes children strong; helps in the digestion of food

Which one of the following statements is correct?

   a Vitamin-C is needed for strong bones.

   b Scurvy is caused due to deficiency of phosphorus.

   c Deficiency of vitamin-C and phosphorus causes rickets.

   d Deficiency of vitamin-D and calcium causes rickets.

24. Given below are some substances given to Anisha.

> (i) Sugar (ii) salt (iii) mustard oil (iv) sand (v) sawdust (vi) honey (vii) chalk powder (viii) petals of flower (ix) soil (x) copper sulphate crystals (xi) glucose

She wants to know whether these substances are soluble in water or not. Help her in identifying them in Group *A*, i.e. soluble and Group B, i.e. insoluble substances in water.

  a Group A–I, II, IV, VI   **b** Group A–I, II, V, VI, VII
      Group B–III, VII, IX, X   Group B–III, VIII, IX, XI
  c Group A–I, II, VI, X, XI   **d** Group A–II, III, IV, V
      Group B–III, IV, VII, IX   Group B–I, VI, VII, VIII

25. Solve the crossword puzzle with the help of clues given below it.

Across

  1. Mineral that helps in blood clotting.
  3. The diet which contains all the nutrients, water and roughage.
  4. Nutrient that repairs the damaged parts of the body.
  5. Nutrient essential for proper functioning of our body.
  6. Animals that eat dead and decaying organic substances.
  8. Animals that eat only flesh of other animals.

Down

  2. Nutrient that gives us energy.
  7. Vitamin good for good eyesight.
  9. Honeybee stores honey in

Chapter 2

Fibre to Fabric

1. Which of the following materials did people use in ancient times for making clothes?

   I. Leaves of trees   II. Newspaper

   III. Metal foils   IV. Animal skins and furs

Choose the correct option

   a I and II   b I and III   c II and III   d I and IV

2. Number of yarns used to make fabric by weaving and knitting are

   a two sets of yarns in each case

   b single yarn in each case

   c two sets of yarns in weaving and single in knitting

   d single yarn in weaving and two sets in knitting

3. Which of the following is the most common source used for wool production in India?

a   b    c    d

4. I am a synthetic fibre. For my preparation you need two chemicals in the ratio of 2 : 5, i.e. dichloride and diaminohexane. Who am I?

   a Rayon   b Nylon

   c Polyester   d Acetate

5. The given figure shows a tool which is used to convert wool fleece into a narrow untwisted fibres called silvers. This tool is used in the process of _____ wool.

   a shearing   b scouring   c carding   d sorting

6. Consider the below terms and opt the correct statement regarding them.

   I : Spinning   II : Reeling

   a I is used in silk production and II is used in wool production

   b I and II both can be used in silk as well as wool production

   c I is used in wool production and II is used in silk production

   d I and II both are optional steps, they are not essential in silk and wool production

7. Larvae of silk moth feed on which part of the mulberry tree?

8. The figure given below shows a stage of life-history of silk moth. Identify which stage is this.

a Eggs on mulberry
b Cocoon
c Cocoon with developing moth
d Pupa developing to silk adult moth

9. Link Column I with Column II.

	Column I		Column II
A.	Cellulose fibre	1.	Flax
B.	Synthetic fibre	2.	Carbon fibre
C.	Inorganic fibre	3.	Nylon
D.	Vegetable fibre	4.	Cellulose ester
E.	Animal fibre	5.	Wool

Codes

	A	B	C	D	E
a	4	1	2	3	5
b	4	3	2	1	5
c	4	2	1	3	5
d	4	5	2	1	3

10. Consider the given statements and opt the best suitable option.

I. They are used for making of wearable dresses.
II. They can be dyed in different colours.
III. They are smooth like silk.
IV. They do not absorb moisture and dry fast.

a Nylon
b Rayon
c Acetate fibres
d Polyester fibres

11. Which of the following factors decide the quality of wool?

A. Thickness   B. Length   C. Shine
D. Strength   E. Colour

a A, B, D
b B, D, E
c C, D, E
d All of these

12. There are some combination given below. Which is the correct match?

	Column I	Column II	Column III
a	Synthetic fibres	Rayon	Weaving
b	Natural fibres	Cotton	Yarns
c	Cotton	Ginning	Fibres
d	Jute	Retting	Separated fibres from rotten stem

13. Which of the following stages in the life-history of a silk moth produces silk fibres?

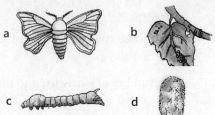
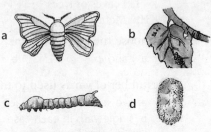

14. Riya described a fabric as following:

I. It absorbs water quickly.
II. It is soft to touch.
III. It creases easily.
IV. It can be washed and ironed easily.
V. It is obtained from plant sources.

Which of the following fibres can form such fabric?

a Cotton
b Silk
c Wool
d Nylon

15. Refer the given flow chart and select the option that correctly identifies the fibres P, Q, R and S.

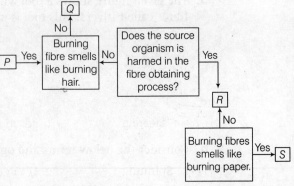

a P – Wool, Q – Silk
b R – Wool, S – Silk
c P – Wool, R – Silk
d Q – Jute, S – Coconut

16. Opt the correct sequence to get cloth.

   a Fibre → Fabric → Yarn
   b Fibre → Yarn → Fabric
   c Fabric → Yarn → Fibre
   d Yarn → Fibre → Fabric

17. Which of the following belongs to silk fibres and its production?

	Protein	Carbohydrate	Reeling	Fleece	Sericulture
a	✓	×	×	×	✓
b	×	✓	✓	×	✓
c	✓	×	✓	×	✓
d	×	×	✓	✓	✓

18. Look at the figures given below. These figures show different steps in the production of wool. A number from (i) to (vi) is written in each block. Find the correct order of the figures.

Knitting | Carding | Dyeing
Spinning | Washing | Shearing

   a (vi), (ii), (iv), (v), (iii), (i)
   b (vi), (v), (ii), (iv), (iii), (i)
   c (v), (vi), (iii), (ii), (iv), (i)
   d (vi), (iii), (ii), (iv), (i), (v)

19. Observe the figure given below and identify the term commonly used for this process.

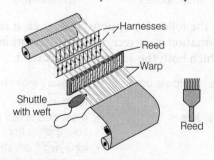

Harnesses
Reed
Warp
Shuttle with weft
Reed

   a Weaving
   b Spinning
   c Knitting
   d Making yarn

20. Identify A, B, C and D in the given flow chart.

A (Boiled or exposed to steam)
↓
B (Taking out threads)
↓
C (Fibres spun into silk threads)
↓
D (Method for fabric or cloth production)

	A	B	C	D
a	Cocoon	Reeling	Silk fabric	Weaving
b	Caterpillar	Spinning	Silk fabric	Sorting
c	Pupa	Shearing	Silk fabric	Weaving
d	Eggs	Burrs	Silk fabric	Scouring

21. Observe the cyclic representation given below of silk formation. Opt the option that correctly declares the time of each phase of the cycle.

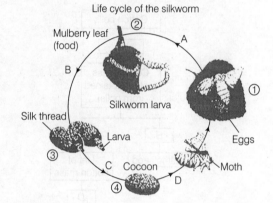

Life cycle of the silkworm

Mulberry leaf (food)
Silkworm larva
B
Silk thread
Larva
Cocoon
Moth
Eggs
A
C
D
①②③④

Codes

	A	B	C	D
a	10 days	4-6 weeks	3-8 days	16 days
b	16 days	3-8 days	4-6 weeks	10 days
c	10 days	3-8 days	4-6 weeks	16 days
d	3-8 days	4-6 weeks	16 days	10 days

22. **Group I** (Fibres) Jute, nylon, leather, wool.

Group II (Properties of nylon) Light weight, strong, absorb water, wrinkle free.

In the above mentioned groups, which member is an exception to it?

	Exception of group I	Exception of group II
a	Wool	Light weight
b	Leather	Absorb water
c	Nylon	Strong
d	Jute	Wrinkle free

23. Match the columns A and B.

	Column A		Column B
I.	Mulberry	i.	To remove burrs from fleece
II.	Organzine	ii.	To soak silk in solutions of salt
III.	Tram	iii.	The best feed for silkworms
IV.	Combing	iv.	Lengthwise thread in silk weaving
V.	Weighting	v.	Crosswise thread in silk weaving

Codes

	I	II	III	IV	V
a	iii	ii	i	iv	v
b	iii	iv	v	i	ii
c	ii	iii	iv	i	v
d	iii	v	iv	ii	i

24. Observe the flow chart given below and mark the part in which ginning process occurs.

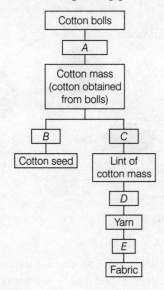

Codes
a Only *B*   b *B* and *C*
c *C* and *E*   d Only *D*

25. Which of the following is the correct sequence of dyeing process?

a Shearing → Scouring → Sorting → Dyeing → Straightening
b Scouring → Shearing → Sorting → Straightening → Dyeing
c Sorting → Shearing → Scouring → Straightening → Dyeing
d Straightening → Shearing → Sorting → Scouring → Dyeing

26. Given below are two groups of materials used to make dress articles.
Group I Jute, cotton
Group II Wool, silk, leather
On what basis, these have been grouped?
a Synthetic fibres   b Natural fibres
c Both (a) and (b)   d None of these

27. Complete the correlation by identifying the correct option at the place of *A*.
I : Silkworm : Cocoon
II : Wool : *A*
Codes
a Spun of sheep   b Cotton
c Fleece of sheep   d Rearing of camel

28. Select the correct match out of the following:

	Sheep breed	Quality of wool	State where found
a	Lohi	Brown fleece	Himachal Pradesh
b	Rampur bushair	Coarse wool	Uttar Pradesh
c	Nali	For hosiery	Gujarat
d	Bakharwali	For woollen shawls	Jammu and Kashmir

29. The states where jute is grown at large level are
a Punjab, Haryana and Rajasthan
b West Bengal, Bihar and Assam
c Karnataka, Kerala and Tamil Nadu
d Madhya Pradesh, Orissa and Uttar Pradesh

30. Which sets of substances is not used for making fibres?
a Silk, chemicals   b Yak hair, camel hair
c Husk, bones   d Flax, wool

31. In the following options, atleast each sentence formation is correct. Identify the option in which both the sentences are correct.

a Cotton is used → as absorbent in hospitals.
→ to spun yarns.

b Jute is → most extensively used fibre than cotton.
→ obtained from stem of plant called 'putson'.

c Examples of natural fibres are → cotton and wool.
→ jute and silk.

d Weaving of fabric is done in → handlooms.
→ takli.

32. Fill in the blanks from the options given below.

(i) fibre	(ii) spring	(iii) retting	(iv) silver
(v) ginning	(vi) rainy	(vii) fabric	(viii) yarn
(ix) spinning	(x) knitting		

I. Separation of fibres from jute stem is called _____ .

II. _____ is pulled and twisted so that the fibre forms a strong thread.

III. Thread like animal or plant tissue is called a _____ .

IV. In _____ season, jute (putson) is cultivated.

V. Cotton is planted in the _____ season.

Codes

	I	II	III	IV	V
a	v	viii	i	ii	vi
b	iii	iv	i	vi	ii
c	x	iv	vii	vi	ii
d	ix	viii	vii	ii	vi

33. Observe the flow chart given below and opt the option that correctly completes the flow chart.

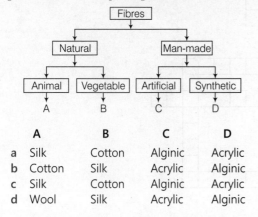

	A	B	C	D
a	Silk	Cotton	Alginic	Acrylic
b	Cotton	Silk	Acrylic	Alginic
c	Silk	Cotton	Alginic	Acrylic
d	Wool	Silk	Acrylic	Alginic

34. Given below are the different breeds of sheep found in various regions. Which of the following is correct for the distribution?

		Punjab	Gujarat	Haryana
a	Nali	×	✓	×
b	Bakharwali	×	✓	×
c	Marwari	×	✓	×
d	Patanwadi	✓	×	×

35. Some words related to fibre to fabric are jumbled up. Opt the correct jumbled and rearranged option.

a GHSEIRNE – SHEERING

b AAORGNE – ANGOERA

c AAAPLC – ALPACA

d RREBLMYA – MALBERRY

36. Steps for the production of silk are given below in an unsequenced manner. Arrange them in a proper sequence.

I. Eggs are warmed to a suitable temperature for the larvae to hatch from eggs.

II. Fibres are taken out from the cocoons

III. After 25 to 30 days, the caterpillars stop eating and start spinning cocoons.

IV. The larvae/caterpillars or silkworms are kept in clean trays along with freshly chopped mulberry leaves.

V. Female silk moths lay eggs.

VI. Cocoons are kept under the sun or boiled in water.

Codes

a	I,	II,	III,	IV,	V,	VI
b	V,	I,	IV,	III,	VI,	II
c	V,	IV,	I,	III,	VI,	II
d	V,	I,	IV,	II,	III,	VI

37. The picture given below is of pashmina shawl. It is of very fine quality and liked by every lady. It is mainly obtained from

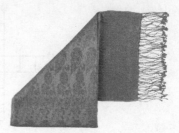

a camel	b goat
c sheep	d yak

38. Consider the passage given below and opt the option that correctly declares them.

Wool industry is an important means of livelihood for many people in our country. But this job is little risky, as sometime the workers get infected by a (1)____ called (2)____ which leads to a fatal (3)____ disease called (4)____.

Codes

	1	2	3	4
a	bacterium	*Bacillus anthracis*	lung	sorter's disease
b	bacterium	*Bacillus*	respiratory	scouring disease
c	fungus	*Salmonella typhimurium*	nasal	asthma
d	virus	*Vibrio anthracis*	skin	skin cancer

39. Consider the given statements and find which one is true or false?

 A. The fur on the body of camels is also used as wool.
 B. Llama and Alpaca found in India yield wool.
 C. Sheep are selectively bred with one parent being a sheep of good breed.
 D. The fleece of the sheep along with a thin layer of skin is removed from its body.
 E. Woollen yarn are processed to obtain woollen fibres.

Codes

	A	B	C	D	E			A	B	C	D	E
a	T	T	T	F	T		b	T	T	T	T	T
c	T	F	T	T	T		d	T	F	T	T	F

40. Assertion (A) Silk production involves cultivation of mulberry leaves and rearing silkworms.
 Reason (R) Scientific name of mulberry is *Morus alba*.
 a Both A and R are true and R is the correct explanation of A
 b Both A and R are true, but R is not the correct explanation of A
 c A is true, but R is false
 d Both A and R are false

41.

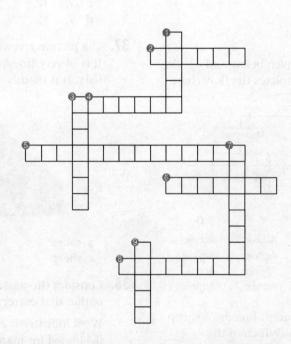

Across
 2. Process of colouring of wool is known as
 5. Food of silkworms
 8. Fleece of sheep is obtained by the process of

3. Silk is obtained from … of silk moth
 6. The first artificial fibre is known as

Down
 1. Variety of silk depends upon.
 7. Cleaning fleece of sheep is

4. Method used for spinning the yarns of wool.
 9. First silk fibre was discovered accidently in

Chapter 3

Sorting and Separation of Materials into Groups

A Sorting Materials into Groups

1. The materials are grouped into various categories on the basis of
   I. similarities and differences in their properties.
   II. nature, size, shape and colour.
   III. solubility, use, transparency and hardness.

   Choose the correct option.
      a Only I   **b** I and II   **c** II and III   **d** All of these

2. Classification means
   I. grouping things as living and non-living.
   II. grouping things on the basis of common properties.
   III. grouping non-living on the basis of common properties.
   IV. grouping all things, living or non-living, on the basis of common properties.

   Choose the correct option.
      a I and II   **b** II and III   **c** Only IV   **d** Only III

3. While playing, Sudhir's coin fell down in a bucket filled with water. He was able to see the coin clearly within the water.

   This is because
      a the water is translucent   **b** the water is transparent
      c the coin is lustrous   **d** the coin is transparent

4. **Assertion** (A) Windshields of cars are made up of glass.
   Reason (R) Those substances through which things are visible are called translucent.
      a Both A and R are true and R is the correct explanation of A
      b Both A and R are true but R is not the correct explanation of A
      c A is true but R is false
      d R is true but A is false

5. Select the row showing correct properties of a liquid.

	Can be compressed	Has a definite shape	Has a definite volume
a	×	×	×
b	✓	×	✓
c	×	✓	✓
d	×	×	✓

Key	✓ Yes
	× No

6. Fill the table by selecting correct word for P, Q, R and S.

Substances

P	Transparent	Q
A substance through which nothing is visible, e.g. *R*.	A substance through which one can see, e.g. water, air.	A substance through which one cannot see clearly, e.g. *S*.

	P	Q	R	S
a	Translucent	Opaque	Milk	Glass
b	Opaque	Translucent	Glass	Milk
c	Translucent	Opaque	Oily paper	Sand
d	Opaque	Translucent	Sand	Oily paper

7. Which of the following objects is made up of one material only?

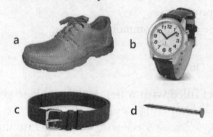

8. Study the classification diagram given below:

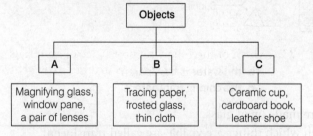

A piece of waxed paper can be grouped under which of the following categories?

  a Only A   b A and B
  c Only C   d B and C

9. What do these things have in common?

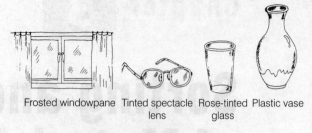

Frosted windowpane   Tinted spectacle lens   Rose-tinted glass   Plastic vase

  I. They are breakable.
  II. They are non-living things.
  III. They are translucent.
  IV. We cannot see through them.

  a I and II   b II and III
  c I, II and IV   d All of these

10. Refer to the classification diagram given below:

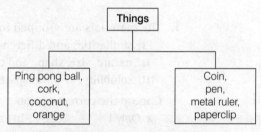

The things are grouped according to

  a how they smell
  b what they are made of
  c where they can be found
  d whether they float or sink in water

11. The part that is marked '*X*' in the diagram given below is copper and it is used because

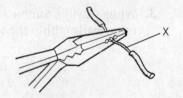

  a it is a precious metal
  b it is an alloy
  c it is a good conductor of electricity
  d it is made of a waterproof material

12. Shaun wants to find out if the rulers of different materials will float or sink.

Which of the following tables correctly shows the most likely observation he has made for this experiment?

Note: The tick (✓) indicates that the object floats on water.

	a		
	Wooden ruler	Metal ruler	Plastic ruler
	✓		✓

	b		
	Wooden ruler	Metal ruler	Plastic ruler
		✓	✓

	c		
	Wooden ruler	Metal ruler	Plastic ruler
		✓	

	d		
	Wooden ruler	Metal ruler	Plastic ruler
	✓	✓	

13. Consider the following substances.

   I. Wood   II. Glass
III. Plastic   IV. Steel
   V. Leather

Which of the above materials are commonly used for making a safety pin?

  a I and II   b II and III
  c III and V   d III and IV

14. While doing an activity in class, the teacher asked Arpita to handover a translucent material. Which among the following materials will Arpita pick and give her teacher?

  a Glass tumbler
  b Mirror
  c Muslin cloth
  d Aluminium foil

15. Consider the following objects.

   I. Chair   II. Table
III. Plough   IV. Bullock cart
  V. Toys   VI. Newspapers
VII. Books

Which of these are not made up of same material?

  a I, III and V
  b VI and VII
  c II, V, VI and VII
  d II, III, IV

16. Which pair of substances among the following would float in a tumbler half-filled with water?

  a Cotton thread, thermocol
  b Feather, plastic ball
  c Pin, oil drops
  d Rubber band, coin

17. Materials/substances are generally grouped
    I. for convenience
   II. to study their properties
  III. for fun
  IV. according to their uses

True statements are

  a I and II   b II, III and IV
  c I, II and IV   d All of these

18. Four students Radha, Sudha, Sofia and Raveena have four different mixtures.

Radha : Red chilli powder + water

Sudha : Butter + water

Sofia : Petrol + water

Raveena : Honey + water

Whose mixture is in solution form?

  a Radha   b Sudha
  c Sofia   d Raveena

19. Complete the following paragraph by selecting appropriate set of words for P, Q, R and S.

P materials are used for making the front glass (windscreen) of a car. Similar property is exhibited by water, in which the P material **Q** Gold is **R** but wood is not. However, both **Q** in **S**.

	P	Q	R	S
a	Opaque	sink	insoluble	soluble
b	Translucent	dissolve	soluble	water
c	Transparent	dissolve	lustrous	water
d	Transparent	sink	lustrous	sand

20. You are provided with the following materials.

   I. Magnifying glass   II. Mirror
III. Stainless steel plate   IV. Glass tumbler

Which of the above materials will you identify as transparent?

  a I and II   b I and III
  c I and IV   d III and IV

21. Which of the following properties of materials should be considered when making a toy boat?

  A. Magnetic material
  B. Ability to float
  C. Waterproof
  D. Ability to allow light to pass through

Codes

  a A and B   b B and C
  c A and C   d C and D

22. Name the kind of material used to make the parts of the car labelled as *X*, *Y* and *Z*.

	X	Y	Z
a	Glass	Plastic	Metal
b	Ceramic	Rubber	Wood
c	Glass	Rubber	Metal
d	Plastic	Metal	Rubber

23. Aman found a bag containing the following materials.

    I. Mirror
    II. Paper stained with oil
    III. Magnet
    IV. Glass spectacles

Help Aman in finding out the material(s) which is/are opaque.

  a Only I   b Only IV
  c I and III   d II and IV

24. Consider the following items.

    I. Glass bowl   II. Plastic toy
    III. Steel spoon   IV. Cotton shirt

Which of the above will shine?

  a I, II and III   b II and III
  c I and III   d III and IV

25. Study the classification diagram given below.

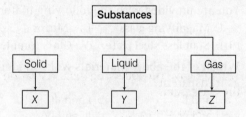

What are the likely objects of *X*, *Y* and *Z*?

	X	Y	Z
a	Chair	Snow	Oxygen
b	Paper	Cough mixture	Watch
c	Plasticine	Water	Steam
d	Hail	Helium	Lotion

26. State 'T' for true and 'F' for false and select the correct option.

    I. Stone is transparent, while glass is opaque.
    II. Chalk dissolves in water.
    III. Oil mixes with water.
    IV. Vinegar dissolves in water.

Codes

	I	II	III	IV
a	F	F	T	F
b	F	F	T	T
c	T	F	T	F
d	F	F	F	F

27. The same object (item) can be made by using different materials. Here with some objects (items) alongwith the materials from which they can be made are given below:

Objects (Items)	Materials			
	Metal	Wood	Plastic	Glass
I. Chair	✓	✓	✓	✗
II. Tea cup	✓	✓	✓	✗
III. Gas cylinder	✗	✓	✓	✗
IV. Pressure cooker	✗	✓	✓	✗

> **Key** ✓ = can be used
>   ✗ = used

Which of the above matchings are incorrect?

  a I and II
  b I, II and III
  c II, III and IV
  d All of the above

28. **Assertion** (A) Pulses (Dal) take the shape of the container in which these are placed.

Reason (R) Liquids take the shape of the container in which these are placed but solids does not.

  a Both A and R are true and R is the correct explanation of A
  b Both A and R are true, but R is not the correct explanation of A
  c A is true, but R is false
  d R is true, but A is false

29. Yen Lin tested the flexibility of 4 identical rubber bands by hanging each from a stand and then adding a weight to it as shown below:

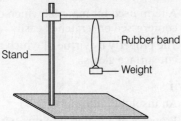

Stand — Rubber band — Weight

She then noted how much each rubber band stretched by measuring its length and recorded her results in a table as shown below:

Rubber band	Length
1	13 cm
2	16 cm
3	11 cm
4	8 cm

Which rubber band is the least flexible?

a 1   b 2   c 3   d 4

30. Study the experiment set-up given below.

 Porcelain Ceramic Glass

Five ice cubes were added to each of the containers. The containers were made up of different materials but were of the same size. Below each container, a candle is used to heat the ice cubes.

The table below shows the results of the experiment.

Material	Time taken for the ice cubes to melt completely
Porcelain	3 min 20 s
Ceramic	5 min 30 s
Glass	1 min 55 s

What is the possible aim of the experiment?

a To find out the flexibility of each material
b To find out if the size of the containers affected the rate of conduction of heat
c To determine if the material of different containers affect the time needed to melt all the ice cubes
d To determine if more candles are needed to conduct the experiment properly

31. Substance 'X' is a good conductor of heat as well as electricity. It is a solid at room temperature and commonly used for making wires. X is

a wood
b copper
c iron
d mercury

32. Mrs Sharma, science teacher of Class VI, write the names of some substances seen in everyday life and classify them in the following manner

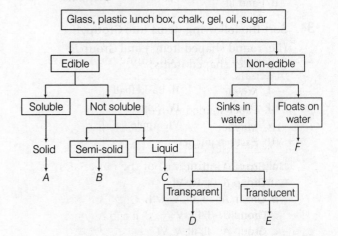

Now, she said to identify A, B, C, D, E and F. The correct identification is

	A	B	C	D	E	F
a	Gel	Sugar	Oil	Chalk	Glass	Plastic lunch box
b	Sugar	Gel	Oil	Chalk	Glass	Plastic lunch box
c	Sugar	Oil	Gel	Glass	Plastic lunch box	Chalk
d	Sugar	Gel	Oil	Glass	Chalk	Plastic lunch box

33. Teacher gave the following demonstration in the classroom.

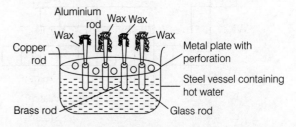

Now, she wrote the following statements as the conclusion of the demonstration and asked the students for selecting correct conclusions.

I. Aluminium is a better conductor of heat as compared to brass.

II. Glass is a better conductor of heat as compared to copper.

III. Aluminium is a better conductor of heat as compared to copper.

IV. Brass is a better conductor of heat as compared to glass.

The correct conclusions are

a I and II
b I and IV
c II and III
d I and III

34. Sort the following items into Group *A* (i.e. round shaped items) and Group *B* (i.e. other shaped items).

I. Water	II. Basketball
III. Orange	IV. Sugar
V. Globe	VI. Apple
VII. Earthen pitcher	

a Group *A* – II, III, V
  Group *B* – I, IV, VI
b Group *A* – II, III, VI, VII
  Group *B* – I, IV, V
c Group *A* – II, III, V, VI
  Group *B* – I, IV, VII
d Group *A* – Only II and III
  Group *B* – All the remaining

35. Complete the following crossword puzzle by filling appropriate words with the help of given clues:

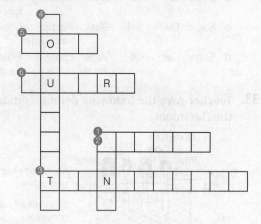

Across

1. A solid which can be squeezed out.
3. We can see through these materials but not clearly.
5. A term used for material which can be compressed or scratched easily.
6. The property by virtue of which a freshly cut surface glows.

Down

2. An insoluble substance.
4. Property of a material to mix with water.

Direction (Q.Nos. 36-38)

Read the following information and answer the questions that follow :

Ravindra collected data about the properties of substances *A, B, C, D, E* and *F* and arranged them in the form of a table as shown below:

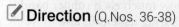

Substance (Material)	Hardness	Transparency	Combustibility	Solubility
A	✓	×	×	×
B	✓	✓	×	×
C	✓	×	✓	✓
D	×	✓	×	✓
E	✓	×	×	✓
F	✓	✓	✓	×

Key ✓ = Yes
× = No

36. Which of the material is most suitable for a shopkeeper for storing different items?

a A   b B
c D   d C

37. Which you will select for making buckets for keeping water?

a A and B   b Only C
c Only A   d E and F

38. Which of the following material can be common salt?

a B and C   b Only E
c Only D   d A and F

B Separation of Substances

1. Match each mixture (given in Column I) to the apparatus (given in Column II) which may be used to separate the components of the mixture.

Column I		Column II
1.	Alcohol and water	A.
2.	Sand and water	B.
3.	Salt and water	C.
4.	Iron filings and sand	D.

	1	2	3	4
a	A	C	B	D
b	B	D	C	A
c	C	A	B	D
d	D	B	A	C

2. Following figure shows the process of purification of river water. Which process is occurring at (1) and (2)?

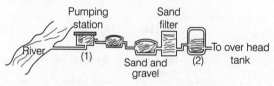

a Sedimentation and filtration
b Filtration and chlorination
c Filtration and sterilisation
d Sedimentation and chlorination

3. Amrita's grandmother is suffering from diabetes. Her doctor advised her to take 'lassi' with less fat content. Which of the following methods would be most appropriate for Amrita to prepare it?

a Filtration   b Decantation
c Churning   d Winnowing

4. Shalu found that there is too much ghee in a particular curry. To remove excess of ghee, she should

a put the curry in the fridge to cool
b remove ghee from top with the help of a ladle
c put the curry in the fridge to cool and then remove ghee from top with the help of a ladle
d None of the above

5. Which method should be adopted to separate the thin film that is formed on prepared and poured tea?

a Filtration   b Decantation
c Sedimentation   d Handpicking

6. Reena wants to boil rice for lunch. She soaks rice in water. She finds that the water above rice level has become opaque. This is because

a the dust and soil get temporarily suspended in water
b rice leaves colour in water
c the water used was dirty
d All of the above

7. Consider the two terms.
X means 'no more will dissolve'.
Y means 'how much will dissolve'.
X and *Y* stands for

a insoluble, amount
b saturated, solubility
c solubility, volume
d insolubility, saturated

8. Consider the following figure.

The above shown technique is used for separating wheat from husk because

a husk is heavier than wheat
b husk is soluble in water
c husk is an undesirable substance
d wheat is heavier than husk

9. Oil + Water $\xrightarrow{\text{Separating funnel}}$ Stirring and stand for some time

Separating funnel
X
Y
Beaker

What would be observation of given separation technique?

a Two distinct layers are formed, in which X is of oil and Y is of water

b Two distinct layers are formed, in which X is of water and Y is of oil

c X and Y are miscible to some extent, so no distinct layers are formed in this experiment

d X and Y mixed to form a homogeneous solution

10. Which is a TRUE statement about water solubility and purifying rock salt with respect to dissolving, filtering, evaporating and crystallising?

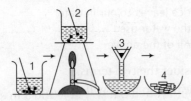

a Salt particles pass through the filter paper because they are so small as compared to the pores of the paper

b Mostly by compounds are less soluble at a higher temperature than at lower temperature

c Solubility data for water are given between 0-100°C because that's the only temperature range we use in laboratory experiments

d All of the above

11. Sonu had a salt solution mixed with sand. To remove sand, he stirred the solution and placed for some time and then decanted. The filtrate still contains some sand. His problem can be solved by

a adding water in excessive amount

b heating the solution

c filtering the solution

d Both (a) and (b)

12. Akshita asked for a glass of water from Arnav. He gave her a glass of ice cold water. Akshita observed some water droplets on the outer surface of the glass and asked Arnav how these droplets of water were formed? Which of the following should be Arnav's answer?

a Evaporation of water from the glass

b Water that seeped out from the glass

c Evaporation of atmospheric water vapour

d Condensation of atmospheric water vapour

13. Read the story titled "Wise Farmer" and tick the correct option to complete the story.

A farmer was happy to see his healthy wheat crop ready for harvest. He harvested the crops and left it under the sun to dry the stalks. To separate the seeds from the bundles of the stalk, he **P**/(I. handpicked , II. threshed) them. After gathering the seed grains, he wanted to separate the stones and husk from it. His wife **Q**/(I. winnowed, II. threshed) them to separate the husk and later **R**/ (I. sieved, II. handpicked) to remove stones from it. She ground the wheat grains and **S**/(I. sieved, II. filtered) the flour. The wise farmer and his wife got a good price for the flour.

	P	Q	R	S
a	I	II	II	I
b	II	I	II	II
c	II	I	II	I
d	II	I	I	II

14. Properties of some substances are tabulated below:

Substance	Appearance	Taste	Magnetic nature	Soluble in water
A	Hard black solid	Salty	No	Yes
B	Light white solid	Sweet	No	No
C	Hard blue solid	No taste	Yes	Yes
D	Hard white solid	Metallic	Yes	No

Which two substances would be most difficult to separate by the use of a magnet?

a A and B   b B and C

c C and D   d A and D

15. In order to check solubility of following substances, Sonia took five test tubes half filled with water and added 1g of

I. salt   II. sand

III. chalk powder   IV. washing powder

V. saw dust and shake well

Then she left them undisturbed for some time. In which cases, she does not get a substance completely soluble in water?

a I and II
b I, II and III
c II, III and V
d III, IV and V

16. Which of the following match is correct?

	Column I	Column II	Column III
a	Muddy water	Sieving	Filtration
b	Tea leaves	Strainer	Decantation
c	Churning of curd	Separation of butter	Filtration
d	Liquid forming the upper layer is carefully poured	Settled solid is left behind	Decantation

17. Consider the following statements:

I. Immiscible liquids are separated by using separating funnel.
II. Before sedimentation, decantation is done.
III. Milk is a mixture.
IV. Winnowing is based on the difference in weights of different substances present in a mixture.

The true statement(s) is/are

a I, II and III
b II, III and IV
c I, III and IV
d I and IV

18. Four mixtures are given below:

I. Kidney beans and chickpeas
II. Pulses and rice
III. Rice flakes and corn
IV. Potato wafers and biscuits

Which of these can be separated by the method of winnowing?

a I and II
b II and III
c I and III
d III and IV

19. During summer, Vipul carries water in a transparent plastic bottle to his school. One day, he left his bottle in the school. The bottle still had some water left in it. The following day, he observed some water droplets on the inner surface of the empty portion of the bottle. These droplets of water were formed due to

a boiling and condensation
b evaporation and saturation
c evaporation and condensation
d condensation and saturation

20. State whether the following statements are true (T) or false (F) and select the correct answer.

I. A mixture of oil and water can be separated by filtration.
II. Water can be separated from salt by evaporation.
III. A mixture of wheat grains and wheat flour can be separated by sieving.
IV. A mixture of iron filings and rice flour can be separated by magnet.
V. A mixture of wheat grains and rice flakes can be separated by winnowing.

	I	II	III	IV	V
a	F	T	T	T	T
b	F	T	F	T	T
c	F	F	T	F	T
d	T	F	T	T	T

21. Sudha found a mixture of iron filings, salt, sand and naphthalene and to separate them, she used some separation techniques which is shown by the following flow chart.

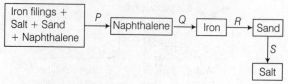

Could you identify P, Q, R and S in above separation scheme?

	P	Q	R	S
a	Sublimation	Magnetic separation	Filtration	Evaporation
b	Magnetic separation	Filtration	Sublimation	Evaporation
c	Evaporation	Magnetic separation	Filtration	Sublimation
d	Sublimation	Magnetic separation	Evaporation	Filtration

22. Consider the following figures.

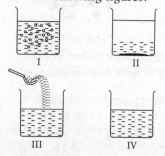

The correct label for I, II, III and IV in the above shown figures is

	I	II	III	IV
a	Suspension	Sediment	Solvent	Solution
b	Suspension	Sediment	Solute	Solution
c	Sediment	Suspension	Solution	Solute
d	Suspension	Sediment	Solute	Solvent

23. The separation of components of a mixture is very important because it is helpful
    I. to separate two or more different but useful components.
    II. to remove undesirable and useless components.
    III. to remove pure or harmless components.
    IV. to obtain pure sample of a substance.

    The true statements are
    a I, II and III
    b I, II and IV
    c II, III and IV
    d I, II, III and IV

24. In an activity, a teacher dissolved a small amount of solid copper sulphate in a tumbler half filled with water.

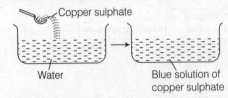

Water   Blue solution of copper sulphate

    Which method would you use to get back solid copper sulphate from the solution?
    a Decantation   b Evaporation
    c Sedimentation   d Condensation

25. Pinki had a mixture of three different substances P, Q and R as shown below:

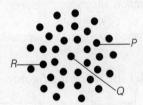

    I. P is heavy and non-magnetic.
    II. Q is magnetic and heavy.
    III. R is light and non-magnetic.

    Which separation technique do you suggest Pinki to separate this mixture?
    a Handpicking followed by filtration
    b Winnowing followed by magnetic separation
    c Magnetic separation followed by sieving
    d Magnetic separation followed by distillation

26. Sonia had a mixture of salt, sand, oil and water. To separate them, she used
    I. evaporation
    II. separating funnel and
    III. filtration

    Arrange these technique in correct sequence to separate the above given mixture.
    a I, II, III   b II, III, I
    c III, I, II   d III, II, I

27. Match the mixtures in Column I with their method of separation in Column II.

	Column I		Column II
A.	Oil mixed in water	1.	Sieving
B.	Iron powder mixed with flour	2.	Handpicking
C.	Salt mixed with water	3.	Decantation
D.	Lady's finger mixed with French beans	4.	Magnet
E.	Rice flour mixed with kidney beans	5.	Evaporation

    Codes
	A	B	C	D	E
a	5	4	3	2	1
b	3	4	5	2	1
c	3	4	5	1	2
d	4	3	5	2	1

28. Consider the following statements.
    I. More salt can be added to saturated solution by heating it.
    II. Heavier substances from the lighter one are separated by threshing.
    III. Precipitation is the process of conversion of water into its vapours.

    The true statement(s) is/are
    a I and II   b I, II and III
    c II and III   d Only I

29. A liquid mixture of three substances A, B and C is separated under following steps:

    Step I The mixture is filtered, so that C gets separated out.

    Step II The filtrate is subjected to distillation. (first boiling and then condensation).

    Step III Then B is collected after condensation and A remain behind in the distillation flask.

Identify *A*, *B* and *C*.

	A	B	C
a	Chalk powder	Water	Saw dust
b	Salt	Water	Sugar
c	Sugar	Water	Sand
d	Saw dust	Water	Sugar

30. John carried out an experiment to find out the effect of salt on the melting point of ice. He wrote down the results in the table below:

Amount of salt added (in g)	0	20	40	60	80
Melting point of ice (°C)	0	− 2	− 4	− 6	− 8

Based on the results given, which of the following statements is correct?
a The melting point of ice when 80 g of salt was added was 0°C
b When more salt was added to the ice, the melting point of ice became higher
c When more salt was added to the ice, the melting point of ice became lower
d There was no effect on the melting point of ice when salt was added

31. Study the diagram below:

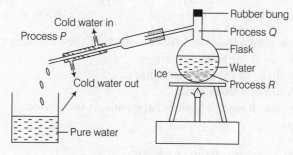

Name the processes that are taking place in *P*, *Q* and *R*.

	P	Q	R
a	Evaporation	Condensation	Melting
b	Condensation	Evaporation	Melting
c	Evaporation	Melting	Condensation
d	Distillation	Condensation	x

32. To separate *P* from *Q*, Rama took the mixture in a China dish and heated it for some time. After that she observed that only *P* remains in the China dish and no traces of *Q* are found.

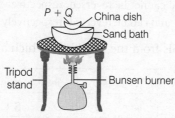

The substances *P* and *Q* and the process *R* are

	P	Q	R
a	Sugar	Salt	Separation
b	Salt	Water	Condensation
c	Water	Salt	Evaporation
d	Salt	Water	Evaporation

Chapter 4

Changes Around Us

1. A list of reversible and irreversible processes was given to VIth grade students. Teacher asked them to separate out reversible processes from the following list.
   - I. Growth of plant
   - II. Stretching of rubber band
   - III. Burning of paper
   - IV. Changing of milk to curd
   - V. Dissolving of salt in water
   - VI. Weathering of rocks

   From the above list reversible processes are
   - a II, IV and VI
   - b II and VI
   - c II and V
   - d II, III and V

2. When air is blown into the balloon, which of the following cases may arise?
   - I. Only size of the balloon changes.
   - II. Only shape of the balloon changes.
   - III. Both size and shape changes.
   - IV. Only size changes whereas shape remains unaffected.

   - a Only I
   - b I and IV
   - c Only III
   - d Only IV

3. Chemical change results in change in
   - I. energy
   - II. colour
   - III. temperature

   The correct option is
   - a I and II
   - b II and III
   - c I, II and III
   - d Only chemical composition

4. Rolling of chapatti and baking of chapatti are the changes that
   - a can be reversed
   - b cannot be reversed
   - c can be reversed and cannot be reversed, respectively
   - d cannot be reversed and can be reversed, respectively

5. Select the five materials from the word box, which are opaque.

A	X	L	T	N	Y	S
R	K	B	O	S	Q	T
P	E	N	C	I	L	O
S	Y	V	O	Z	T	N
Q	M	D	A	R	P	E
Z	F	N	L	E	A	F

6. Rashmi took a beaker filled with water. She cover this beaker with a metal plate. Then she boiled the water with the help of a Bunsen burner as shown below.

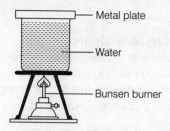

She then removed the burner and left the beaker as such. After a few minutes, what was her observation?

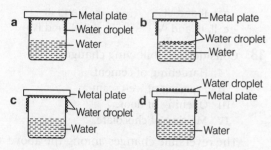

7. Boojho's sister broke a white dove, a symbol of peace, made of plaster of Paris (POP). Boojho tried to reconstruct the toy by making a powder of the broken pieces and then making a paste by mixing water. Will he be successful in his effort and why?

   a Yes, because it involves only a physical change, i.e. chemical composition remains unaffected

   b Yes, because it involves the formation of a new substance

   c No, because of the formation of a new substance having properties different from the original POP

   d No, because such a change is reversible in nature

8. Iron rim is made slightly smaller than the wooden wheel (which is to be covered by iron rim). The rim is usually heated before fixing into the wooden wheel because on heating, the iron rim

   a expands and fits onto the wooden wheel

   b contracts and fits onto the wooden wheel

   c no change in the size takes place

   d expands first, then on cooling contracts and fits onto the wooden wheel

9. Study the following venn diagram.

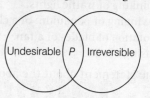

P is

   a burning of cooking gas

   b coming of summer

   c mixing of sugar and milk

   d an earthquake

10. Water on heating converts into steam(gas) and on freezing at about 0°C converts into ice (solid). Both the changes are reversible and are called physical changes because

   a a physical change include the formation of a new substance with different properties

   b a physical change involve no change in colour and all the three are colourless

   c a physical change does not affect the chemical composition

   d All of the above

11. Consider the following phenomena.

   I. Boiling of water.

   II. Melting of ice.

   III. Freezing of water.

Which of the above take place with the evolution of energy?

   a I and II

   b II and III

   c I and III

   d Only III

12. Consider the following phenomena.

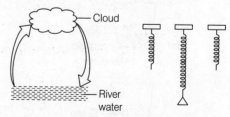

What types of changes are taking place in the above figures?

   a Physical and chemical respectively

   b Physical and reversible respectively

   c Chemical and reversible respectively

   d Physical and irreversible respectively

13. Consider the following phenomena.
   I. Blinking of traffic lights.
   II. Swinging of pendulum of a clock.
   III. Rotation of blades of a fan.
   IV. Rising of sun.

The true statement about the above changes is
   a All are physical changes
   b All are chemical changes
   c All are periodic changes
   d All are irreversible changes

14. Ravi took a piece of cloth and cut it into several small pieces. He hold a piece with the help of tongs and burn it.

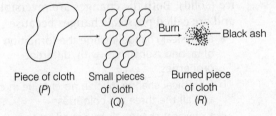

Piece of cloth (P)   Small pieces of cloth (Q)   Burned piece of cloth (R)

The correct statement about the above conversion process is
   a $P \rightarrow Q$ is a reversible change but $Q \rightarrow R$ is irreversible change
   b $P \rightarrow Q$ is a reversible change and $Q \rightarrow R$ is also reversible change
   c $P \rightarrow Q$ is an irreversible change and $Q \rightarrow R$ is also irreversible change
   d $P \rightarrow Q$ is an irreversible change and $Q \rightarrow R$ is reversible change

15. Seema had a blue colour solution of blue vitriol but after a few days, she found that it turns green. She also found a iron nail there was in the solution.

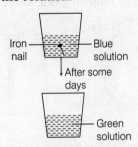

Conversion of blue solution into green is a
   a physical and reversible change
   b physical and irreversible change
   c chemical and reversible change
   d chemical and irreversible change

16. Study the venn diagram carefully.

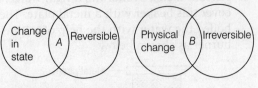

A and B respectively are
   a breaking of wooden sticks, evaporation
   b breaking of brick, melting of ice
   c breaking of brick, freezing of water
   d freezing of water, breaking of brick

17. Formation of curd from milk is a
   I. temporary change   II. irreversible change
   III. chemical change   IV. exothermic change

The correct alternative is
   a I, II and III   b II and III
   c II, III and IV   d I, III and IV

18. Consider the following changes.
   I. Hardening of cement.
   II. Freezing of ice-cream.
   III. Opening of door.
   IV. Melting of chocolate.

The reversible changes among the above are
   a I, II and III   b II, III and IV
   c III and IV   d I, II and IV

19. Complete the following paragraph by selecting a set of appropriate words from the given options:

Blacksmith generally make their own tools from iron. For this, they heated a piece of iron till it becomes _P_. It then becomes _Q_ and is beaten into a desired shape. On _R_, it again becomes _S_.

	P	Q	R	S
a	red hot	hard	cooling	soft
b	cooling	hard	red hot	soft
c	cooling	soft	red hot	hard
d	red hot	soft	cooling	hard

20. Paheli lighted a candle and observed the following changes.
   I. Wax was melting.
   II. Candle was burning.
   III. Size of the candle was reducing.
   IV. Melted wax was getting solidified.

Of the above, the changes that can be reversed are
   a I and II   b II and III
   c III and IV   d I and IV

21. Assertion (A) Dissolution of salt into water is a physical change.

Reason (R) A physical change does not affect the chemical composition of the substance taking part in the change.

    a Both A and R are true and R is the correct explanation of A

    b Both A and R are true, but R is not the correct explanation of A

    c A is true, but R is false

    d R is true, but A is false

22. Consider the following flow chart.

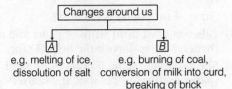

A and *B* stand respectively for

    a reversible and irreversible changes

    b chemical and physical changes

    c permanent and temporary changes

    d All of the above

23. Ravina take an iron ring and heat it.

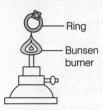

After that she cooled it.

The observation of this experiment as assumed by Ravina are as follow:

  I. The ring expands.

  II. The ring almost comes to the same size on cooling.

  III. The change in this case is reversed.

  IV. The ring changes its shape and the change cannot be reversed.

The true observations are

    a I, II and III

    b II, III and IV

    c I, III and IV

    d All of the above

24. Match the Column I with Column II and choose the correct answer using the codes given below.

	Column I		Column II
p.	Burning of candle.	i.	Undesirable
q.	Souring of milk.	ii.	Physical as well as chemical
r.	Glowing of electric lamp.	iii.	Natural
s.	Tsunami	iv.	Physical

Codes

	p	q	r	s
a	ii	i	iv	iii
b	i	ii	iv	iii
c	ii	iv	i	iii
d	ii	i	iii	iv

25. Consider the following statements.

  I. Formation of dew is a physical change.

  II. Explosion of bombs is an endothermic process.

  III. Dissolution of common salt can be reversed by heating.

The true statements are

    a I and II   b I and III

    c II and III   d I, II and III

26. Sobhita, science teacher of Class VI, write the following statements and ask one word for these statements from the students.

The statements written by Sobhita and answers given by the students are as follow.

	Statements	Answers
I.	A change like rusting of iron.	Fast change, reversible
II.	A non-useful change for man.	Undesirable change
III.	A change which have no effect on chemical composition.	Physical change
IV.	A change which is irreversible in nature.	Physical change

The true answers are

    a I and II   b II and III

    c I, II and III   d I, II, III and IV

27. Consider the following statements about a chemical change.

  I. It is a permanent and irreversible change.

  II. In this, heat or light is either evolved or absorbed.

  III. It results in the formation of no new substance.

  IV. The properties of original substance are different from the substance formed.

The true statements are

    a I, II and III   b II, III and IV

    c I, II and IV   d All of these

28. Rama took a needle and try to magnetised it.

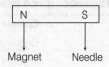

Some statements about this change are

   I. It is a permanent change.
   II. It is a chemical change.
   III. It is reversible in nature.

The true statement(s) is/are

   a Only I   b Only III
   c II and III   d I, II and III

29. State 'T' for true and 'F' for false and select the correct answer.

   I. Physical changes do not affect the colour of the substance.
   II. Formation of coal is an example of a natural change.
   III. No exchange of energy takes place in a physical change.
   IV. Rusting of iron is a fast chemical change.

   Codes

	I	II	III	IV
a	T	T	F	F
b	T	F	T	F
c	F	F	T	T
d	F	T	T	F

30. A potter makes a clay pot on the potter's wheel. He then bakes the clay pot. Which of the following statements regarding this are correct?

   a Baking of clay pot is an irreversible change
   b Making of clay pot is a reversible change
   c Both the changes require energy
   d All of the above

31. Raveena's mother took some gram flour (basen) and made its dough. She make chapatti from the dough and rolled them. Then she boiled the rolls in water and cut them into pieces. The above process can be represented in the form of following flow chart.

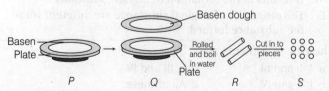

What types of changes are involved in the conversion of P into Q, Q into R and R into S?

	$P \to Q$	$Q \to R$	$R \to S$
a	Physical	Physical	Physical
b	Physical	Chemical	Chemical
c	Chemical	Chemical	Physical
d	Physical	Chemical	Physical

32. It was Paheli's birthday, her brother Simba was helping her to decorate the house for the birthday party and their parents were also busy making other arrangements. Following were the activities going on at Paheli's home:

   (i) Simba blew balloons and put them on the wall.
   (ii) Some of the balloons got burst.
   (iii) Paheli cut colourful strips of paper and put them on the wall with the help of tape.
   (iv) She also made some flowers by origami (paper folding) to decorate the house.
   (v) Her father made dough balls.
   (vi) Mother rolled the dough balls to make *puries*.
   (vii) Mother heated oil in a pan.
   (viii) Father fried the *puries* in hot oil.

Sort out the above activities into Group I (i.e. the changes that can be reversed) and Group II (i.e. the changes which cannot be reversed).

   a Group I -- (i), (iii), (iv), (vii)
     Group II –   ., (v), (vi), (viii)
   b Group I – (i), (iii), (iv), (v), (vi)
     Group II – (ii), (viii), (vii)
   c Group I – (ii), (iii), (v), (vii)
     Group II – (i), (iv), (vi), (viii)
   d Group I – (iv) and (v)
     Group II – All except (iv) and (v)

✓ **Direction** (Q. Nos. 33-35)

A metal ring has to be fixed on a wooden wheel. The blacksmith heats the metal ring and puts it on the wheel. The wheel fits perfectly after some time.

33. The metal ring that was fixed on the wheel was

    a of the same size as the wheel   **b** of a size slightly smaller than the wheel

    c of a bigger size than the wheel   **d** None of these

34. The metal ring undergoes _____ .

    a no change   **b** chemical change

    c irreversible change   **d** reversible change

35. A piece of iron can be used to make different kinds of tools. This is because

    a iron is a metal and quite malleable   **b** heating causes a reversible change

    c hot iron is soft and can be reshaped   **d** All of these

36. Fill the following crossword puzzle with the help of hints given below.

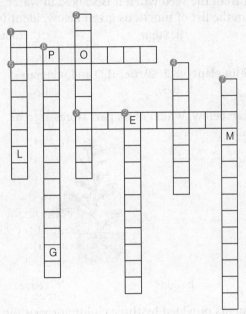

Across

    3. A change which can be inverted is called.   6. An example of chemical change is this.

Down

    1. A change useful for man is called _____ change.

    2. A change occurring with the absorption of energy is called _____ change.

    4. Change of season is such kind of change.

    5. Explosion is such type of change.

    7. A change resulting in the formation of a new substance.

    8. An another term used for temporary change.

Chapter 5

Getting to Know Plants

1. I come out first from the seed when it is soaked in water. I provide anchorage to plants. Who am I? From the list of functions given below, identify its function.

    A. Leaves   B. Stem   C. Roots

Functions

    1. Make food for plant   2. Carries H_2O and minerals   3. Absorbs H_2O and minerals

    a A-1   **b** B-3   **c** C-2   **d** D-3

2. In the plant given below, which of its part stores starch?

    a Flower   **b** Buds   **c** Leaves   **d** Stem

3. Read the statements provided by three children about the roots of plants.

Navya : All roots grow underground.

Purvi : Some roots provide us with food.

Ravi : Roots that grow underground tend to grow downwards.

Who made correct statement(s) about roots?

    a Navya   **b** Navya and Purvi   **c** Navya and Ravi   **d** Purvi and Ravi

4. Look at the figure of a plant below.

Which of the following statements about the plant is correct?

    A. This plant has a weak stem.   B. This plant is a flowering plant.

    C. This plants uses the trunk of a tree for support. D. This plant has a thick and woody stem.

Codes

    a A and C   **b** C and D   **c** A, B and D   **d** A, C and D

5. Read what Avi describes about the plant that he has in his garden.

It is a land plant. It has flowers. It has hard and woody stem

Which of the following is likely to be the plant that Avi is describing?
a Rose
b Sandalwood
c Passion flower
d Sunflower

6. Look at the tree below.

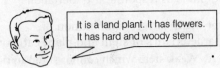

What is the importance of the part labelled *X*?
A. It helps the plant to make food.
B. It acts as a hard covering to protect inner parts of a tree.
C. It prevents the tree from losing too much water from evaporation.
D. It carries the food to other parts of the plant.
E. It holds the plant upright.

Codes
a A and B
b B, D and E
c C, D and E
d A and E

7. Which of the following statements about plants are true?
A. All plants are edible.
B. Plants are green because of the presence of chlorophyll.
C. A shrub is also known as a tree.
D. The stem of a cactus is green and contains chlorophyll.

a B and D
b A, B and D
c B, C and D
d A, B, C and D

8. Plant *A* is different from plant *B* because_____.

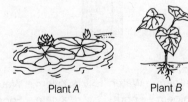

Plant *A*   Plant *B*

a it is a flowering plant.
b it has flowers that grow in a bunch.
c its leaves are jagged.
d its roots need to take in more water for the plant.

9. Which of the following is correct for plants? ($\uparrow$ – upward movement, $\downarrow$ – downward movement).

	Water	Minerals	Food
a	$\uparrow$	$\uparrow\downarrow$	$\uparrow$
b	$\uparrow$	$\downarrow$	$\downarrow$
c	$\downarrow\uparrow$	$\downarrow$	$\downarrow\uparrow$
d	$\uparrow$	$\uparrow$	$\downarrow\downarrow$

10. Which of the following plants show tap root systems?

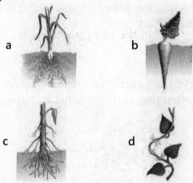

11. Observe the figure given below and opt the options that correctly states its features.

a Parallel venation and fibrous root
b Parallel venation and tap root
c Reticulate venation and fibrous root
d Reticulate venation and tap root

12. The diagram below shows various stages as a seed germinates into a young plant.

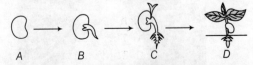

A   B   C   D

At which stage(s) does the germinating seed need to take in oxygen?
a Only D
b C and D
c A, B and C
d A, B, C and D

Direction (Q. nos. 13-14)

The following experiment was carried out to compare the growth of seeds.

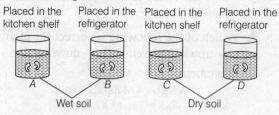

Placed in the kitchen shelf   Placed in the refrigerator   Placed in the kitchen shelf   Placed in the refrigerator

A   B   C   D

Wet soil   Dry soil

13. In which of the above set ups, will the seeds grow first?

   a A
   c C
   b B
   d D

14. In which of the above set ups will the seeds not grow at all?

   a A and B
   c A, B and C
   b B and D
   d B, C and D

15. Observe the figure given below and opt the option that correctly label its parts.

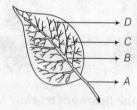

Codes

	A	B	C	D
a	Vein	Lamina	Mid-rib	Petiole
b	Lamina	Vein	Mid-rib	Petiole
c	Petiole	Vein	Mid-rib	Lamina
d	Petiole	Mid-rib	Lamina	Vein

16. Look at the figure of an activity given below. In this, a process is carried out with leaves of plant and polythene bag. Which process is being studied in the activity?

Codes

   a Photosynthesis
   c Stimulus response
   b Transpiration
   d Guttation

17. Opt the incorrect combination of characteristics of stem and plant category?

   A. Weak stem which cannot stand upright : Creeper

   B. Green tender stem : Shrub

   C. Thick, hard stem with branching near the base : Tree

   D. Thick, hard stem with branching high : Herb on the plant

Codes

   a A and B
   c C and D
   b B and C
   d All except A

18. Read the parts given below, categorise then as male and female part of the flower.

   1. Anther   2. Ovule
   3. Pollen grain   4. Ovary
   5. Filament   6. Style
   7. Stamen   8. Pistil

Choose the correct option.

	Male	Female
a	1, 3, 5 and 6	2, 4, 7 and 8
b	2, 4, 6 and 7	1, 3, 5 and 8
c	1, 3, 5 and 7	2, 4, 6 and 8
d	1, 2, 3 and 5	4, 6, 7 and 8

19. Which of the following figures shows the reticulate type of venation in a leaf?

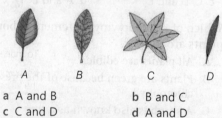

A   B   C   D

   a A and B
   c C and D
   b B and C
   d A and D

20. Look at the figure of transportation mechanism and identify which part is this and what does it transports?

   a Phloem – Water
   c Phloem – Food
   b Xylem – Water
   d Xylem – Food

21. Which of the following combination is correct?

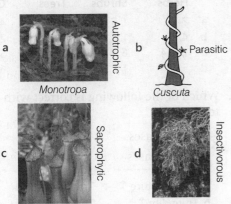

a Monotropa — Autotrophic
b Cuscuta — Parasitic
c Pitcher plant — Saprophytic
d Lichen on a pine tree — Insectivorous

22. Which of the following is correct for a plant?

	Adaptation	Function
A.	Stomata	allow CO_2 to diffuse in and O_2 to diffuse out
B.	Epidermal cells	allow sunlight to penetrate to the mesophyll layer
C.	Chloroplast containing chlorophyll	absorb sunlight for making food
D.	Xylem tubes	to take away sucrose

Codes
a A and B
b B and C
c C and D
d A, B and C

23. A table of mineral ions required by plants is given under: Identify A and B.

	Nitrogen	Magnesium
Mineral salt	Nitrates or ammonium ions	Magnesium ions
Why needed	To make A	To make B
Deficiency	Weak growth, yellow leaves	Yellowing between the veins of leaves

Codes

	A	B
a	Carbohydrates	CO_2
b	Protein	Carbohydrates
c	Protein	Chlorophyll
d	Protein	Chloroplast

24. Consider the statements given below
I. Plants are unicellular.
II. Plants are heterotrophs.
III. Plants respond to environment.
IV. Plants prepare their own food.

Which of the above statements are correct?
a II and IV
b III and IV
c Only IV
d I, II, III and IV

25. What are the basic conditions required for a plant to grow from a seed to an adult plant?

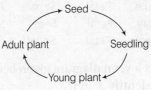

A. type of air
B. kind of fertiliser
C. amount of water
D. optimum temperature

a A and B
b C and D
c B and C
d B, C and D

26. The graph shows the growth of a bean seed over a period of time. Which of the following is true?

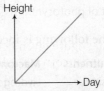

a The bean plant is dying.
b The bean plant is growing at a 45° angle.
c The bean plant is growing strong and healthy.
d The bean plant remains at the same height over the period of time.

27. I. Roots $\xrightarrow{A}$ leaves

II. Leaves $\xrightarrow{B}$ rest of the plant
In the above equations, what is A and B?
To what A and B relate?

Codes

	A	Relation	B	Relation
a	Water	– Phloem;	Food	– Phloem
b	Water	– Xylem;	Food	– Phloem
c	Water	– Phloem;	Water	– Xylem
d	Water	– Xylem;	Food	– Xylem

28. Observe the figure given below and choose the correct option by identifying P, Q, R, S.

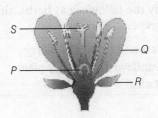

Codes

	P	Q	R	S
a	Ovary	Sepal	Petal	Style
b	Ovule	Petal	Sepal	Pistil
c	Ovary	Petal	Sepal	Style
d	Ovary	Petal	Sepal	Stigma

29. There is a venn diagram given below. Observe it and identify X in it?

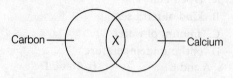

Codes
a Micronutrient
b Macronutrient
c Product of respiration
d Product of photosynthesis

30. Which of the following is incorrect?

	Micronutrients	Macronutrients
a	Magnesium, boron, carbon	Hydrogen, iron, phosphorus
b	Hydrogen, carbon, magnesium	Calcium, zinc
c	Magnesium, iron	Hydrogen, carbon, chlorine
d	Nitrogen, sulphur, iron	Hydrogen, nitrates boron

31.

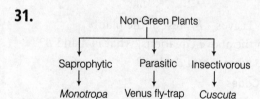

Observe and analyse the above flow chart and find the incorrect categorisation.
a *Monotropa* is incorrectly placed in the flow chart
b Both venus fly-trap and *Cuscuta*
c Only *Cuscuta*
d All of the above

32. Classify the following as herbs, shrubs, trees and creepers.

1. Jasmine	2. Strawberry	3. Mango
4. Sunflower	5. Money plant	6. Rose
5. Radish	8. Tulsi	

Choose the correct option.

	Herbs	Shrubs	Trees	Creepers
a	2, 5	1, 6	3, 8	4, 7
b	4, 7	1, 6, 8	3	2, 5
c	1, 2, 4	6, 7	3	5, 8
d	5, 8	1, 2, 4	3	6, 7

33. Which of the following is correct with respect to plants?

Key	↑ Increases
	↓ Decreases

a Temperature ↑ – Transpiration ↓
b Humidity ↑ – Transpiration ↓
c Wind speed ↑ – Transpiration ↓
d Water supply ↑ – Transpiration ↓

34. Which of the following option is correct on the basis of the presence or absence of flower?

	Wheat	Tulsi	Peepal	Banyan
a	✓	✓	✗	✓
b	✓	✓	✓	✗
c	✗	✗	✗	✗
d	✓	✓	✓	✓

35. I : Root II : Stem
Consider the above parts and identify the correct statement.
a II of sweet potato stores food but its II does not
b I of ginger stores food but its II does not
c I and II of pulses store food
d All statements are correct

36. Which of the following statements are correct?
A. Anther is a part of the stamen.
B. The visible parts of a bud are the petals.
C. Lateral roots are present in a tap root.
D. Leaves perform the function of transpiration and photosynthesis.

Codes
a A and B   b A, C and D
c C and D   d A, B, C and D

37.

A.   B.

C.   D.

Which of the following shows the correct order to growth of a seed to an adult plant?

a B, C, D, A   b C, A, D, B
c D, B, C, A   d A, C, B, D

38. Seeds require _____ to grow well.

A. Air   B. Water
C. Fertilisers   D. Chlorophyll
E. Humidity   F. pH
G. Natural agent

Codes

a A, B and E   b A, B, C, E, F and D
c A, C, F, D and G   d A, B, C and D

39. Consider the given passage and opt the option that correctly fill in the blanks.

Stamen is made up of ___A___ and ___B___. It represents the ___C___ part of the flower. The female part of the flower is called the ___D___. The basal, swollen part of the pistil is called the ___E___ which contains the ___F___.

Codes

	A	B	C	D	E	F
a	petals	pistil	bud	pistil	anther	food
b	petals	style	filament	ovary	ovule	seed
c	petals	pistil	male	ovary	ovule	pollen
d	filament	anther	male	pistil	ovary	ovule

40. There is an activity given below. Analyse this activity and opt the option that correctly declares the objective behind it.

  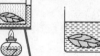

Leaf in boiling water Step I   Leaf in water at room temperature Step II   Leaf in alcohol heated in a water bath Step III   Leaf in iodine solution Step IV

Codes

a Rate of photosynthesis
b The presence of starch
c The presence of cellulose in cell wall
d Strength of plant

41. Match the column I with column II.

	Column I		Column II
A.	Veins	1.	Attachment of leaf to stem
B.	Margin	2.	Green flat part of leaf
C.	Lamina	3.	Gives shape to the leaf
D.	Petiole	4.	Transport water, mineral and food
E.	Reticulate venation	5.	Tap root
		6.	Fibrous root

Codes

	A	B	C	D	E
a	3	4	2	1	6
b	4	3	2	1	5
c	1	4	3	2	5
d	1	2	3	4	6

42. Consider the statements given below about photosynthesis and opt the correct statements.

I. Sunlight, carbon dioxide, chlorophyll and water are necessary components of photosynthesis process.
II. Oxygen is absorbed during the process.
III. Leaves carry out photosynthesis.
IV. Proteins are made during photosynthesis.

Codes

a III and IV   b II and IV
c I and III   d I and IV

43. There are some names of flowering plants having either joined sepals or separated sepals. Opt the correct categorised option.

	Joined sepals	Separated sepals
a	Datura and gurhal	Loki and mustard
b	Loki and mustard	Datura and gurhal
c	Datura and Loki	Gurhal and mustard
d	Gurhal and mustard	Datura and loki

44. We have taken the lowermost and swollen part of the pistil and cut it longitudinally and transversely. Now, it looks like as shown in the figure given below. Name the part labelled as *X* ?

a Style   b Ovary   c Stigma   d Ovule

45. Observe the figure given alongside. Accordingly opt the option that describes what will not occur in *B*, but occur in *A*, on the immediate hour after digging them into the soil.

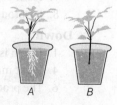

Codes

a *A* will absorb water, but *B* will not.
b *A* will absorb oxygen from air, but *B* will not.
c Both can absorb water and oxygen.
d *A* will absorb carbon dioxide but *B* will not.

46.
A. Rise   B. Tomato   C. Blueberry   D. *Camellia*
E. Rosemary   F. China rose   G. Lavender

The above plants are either herb or shurb. Categorise them correctly by opting correct option.

Herb	Shurb		Herb	Shurb
a A, B and C	D, E, F and G	b	C, D, F and G	A, B and E
c A, B, E and G	C, D and F	d	A, B, E, F and G	C and D

47. Assertion (A) Plants have a tendency to prepare their own food.

Reason (R) Plants perform a process called transpiration.
a Both A and R are true and R is the correct explanation of A
b Both A and R are true, but R is not the correct explanation of A
c A is correct, but R is false
d Both A and R are false

48. Solve the below crossword with the help of given hints.

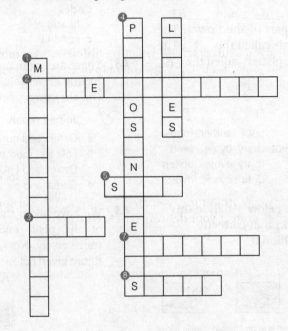

Across
2. Plants that eat insects are called as _____.
3. Plants absorb water and minerals from the soil through _____ .
5. Xylem and phloem tissues in _____ help to transport essential substances.
7. Plant organ that helps in transpiration.
8. By-product of photosynthesis.

Down
1. Boron is classified as _____ (type of nutrient).
4. Plant makes sugar by the process of _____.
6. The process in takes place in _____.

Chapter 6

Body Movements

1. There are some organisms given below. Which of these organisms have a skeletal system?

    I. Jellyfishes   II. Earthworms

    III. Snake   IV. Mouse

    Codes

    a Only I   b II and IV   c I and II   d III and IV

2. Observe the given venn diagram depicting different body movement a postures and identify 'X' (a joint or a bone) with the help of given options.

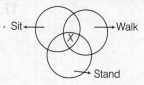

    a Pelvic gridle   b Ribcage   c Ball and socket joint   d Tendon

3. I give you shape. Without me, you are like jelly. I give you support like the pillars of a building. I also protect your delicate parts. Who am I?

    a Tissue   b Cell wall   c Skeleton   d Muscle

4. Given below is a flow diagram for a major system in our body. Choose the option that fills the missing links A, B, C correctly

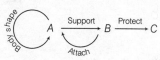

    Codes

	A	B	C		A	B	C
a	Tendons	Bones	Muscles	b	Bones	Muscles	Organs
c	Organs	Muscles	Bones	d	Muscles	Bones	Organs

5. Identify A, B and C in the table given below.

A	B	C
Connects bone to bone	Connects muscle to bone	Form temporary skeleton
Provide stability	Allows movement	Provide flexibility
e.g. wall of eye to lens	e.g. calf muscle to heel	e.g. our external ear

    Codes

	A	B	C		A	B	C
a	Bone	Muscle	Tendon	b	Tendon	Ligament	Cartilage
c	Ligament	Tendon	Cartilage	d	Cartilage	Tendon	Ligament

6. Given below are some structures of human body. Pick the odd one out.

a Ball and socket   b Pivot
c Hinge   d Sternum

7. Consider the given below statements.

   I. A baby has 300 bones in his body.
   II. Bones of our body act as a framework or give it shape.
   III. There are twenty two muscles that make up the skull.
   IV. Coccyx is called the tail bone.
   V. Hip bone is formed by the fusion of two bones.

Which of the above statements are correct?

a I, II, III and V   b I, II and IV
c II, III, IV and V   d I, II, III, IV and V

8. Which of the following is correct?

	Part of the body	Number of bones
A.	Head	22
B.	Forelimb	30
C.	Hindlimb	30
D.	Ribs	26
E.	Vertebral column	24
F.	Hip	3

Codes

a A, B, C and F   b D, E and F
c A, B, C and E   d All are correct

9. A human skeleton is given below. Observe and choose the option that label its part correctly.

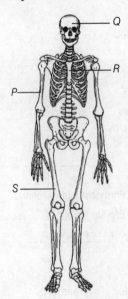

	P	Q	R	S
a	Ulna	Mandible	Scapula	Tibia
b	Humerus	Cranium	Sternum	Femur
c	Humerus	Mandible	Sternum	Femur
d	Ulna	Cranium	Scapula	Tibia

10. Given below are some statements and their related terms. Choose the correct pairs.

	Statements	Related terms
A.	Bone that together with the radius forms the forearm	Ulna
B.	Largest bone in the body	Tibia
C.	Skeleton of the head including cranium	Skull
D.	Structure that supports lower limbs in humans	Pelvis

Codes

a A and B   b B and C
c A, C and D   d None of these

11. Consider the statements given below and identify the term that justify these statements.

   A. It work like a penknife.
   B. In this type of joint, the slightly bulging surface of one bone fits into the depressed surface of another bone.
   C. It allows movement only in one direction.

Codes

a Ball and socket joint
b Hinge joint
c Pivot joint
d Gliding joint

12. Observe the figure given below

Which of the following is the correct description of X?

a X is called the tail bone and consist of four bones that fuse together as one grows up.
b X is called the sacrum and consist of four bones.
c X is called lumber. It provide balance to the pelvic region.
d X is the only bone not connected to another.

13. Consider the labellings given below.

    I. Ball and socket joint.

    II. Hinge joint.

    Which of the following is correct?

    A. I allow greatest freedom of movement but II allow movement only in one direction.

    B. I allow movement at 90° only but II allow movement only in 180°.

    C. I is present in shoulder and II is present in knee.

    D. I allow a person to stretch his muscles but II dont.

Codes

  a A and B

  b A and C

  c B and C

  d C and D

14. There are three groups given below. Observe each group and identify the correct relation with other groups.

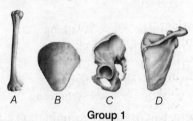

Group 1

Irregular bone	Short bone	Flat bone	Long bone
P	Q	R	S

Group 2

Upper and lower arm	Wrist bone	Bone of cranium	Vertebrae protects the spinal cord
M	N	O	T

Group 3

Codes

  a A–R–M, B–Q–M, C–S–T, D–P–O

  b A–Q–N, B–P–O, C–R–N, D–S–T

  c A–P–O, B–R–T, C–Q–M, D–S–N

  d A–S–M, B–Q–N, C–P–T, D–R–O

15. Human skull is shown below. Opt the correct number of the total bones of skull and facial bones, respectively.

Human skull

	Total bones	Facial bones
a	22	14
b	20	12
c	22	11
d	14	7

16. A boy in the figure below is exercising. He lifts his hand in up and down position. Which of the following union of bones help in lifting hand?

Codes

  a Clavicle, humerus and scapula

  b Clavicle, sternum and humerus

  c Fibula, patella and scapula

  d Fibula, patella and humerus

17. Match the column I with column II.

	Column I		Column II
A.		1.	Pivot joint
B.		2.	Saddle joint
C.		3.	Ball and socket joint
D.		4.	Plane joint
E.		5.	Hinge joint

Codes

	A	B	C	D	E
a	1	2	3	4	5
b	5	3	4	1	2
c	5	1	2	3	4
d	5	4	3	1	2

18. Boats and ships are designed to move efficiently through water. Their shape is similar to fishes. From the options below, choose the correct combination of shape and its advantage.

Shape		Advantage	
1.	Cylindrical	A.	Provide wave motion
2.	Streamlined	B.	Increases water resistance
3.	Circular	C.	Decreases water resistance
4.	Conical	D.	Helps in ballooning

Codes

a 1–B   b 2–C   c 3–D   d 4–A

19. Muscles and bones work together to move various parts of our body, in order to bring movement. In the figure given below, arms in two condition have been shown. One is in straight position and other in bending. Identify X, Y, P and Q in the figure with the help of options that follow.

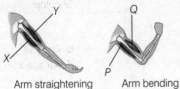

Arm straightening   Arm bending

Codes

	X	Y	P	Q
a	Relaxing	Contracting	Contracting	Relaxing
b	Contracting	Relaxing	Relaxing	Contracting
c	Contracting	Contracting	Relaxing	Contracting
d	Relaxing	Contracting	Contracting	Contracting

20. A boy fell off a tree and hurt his ankle. On examination the doctor confirmed that the ankle was fractured. Which of the following help in the examination of fracture?

	Symptom	Confirmation
a	Swelling on ankle	By X-ray
b	Redness on ankle	By CT scan
c	Swelling and redness	By visual appearance
d	Swelling and pain	By X-ray and visual appearance

21. Observe the figure A and B, given below that show skeleton of a bird well-suited for flying. There some statements are also given.

A   B

Statements

I. The bones of birds are hollow and light.

II. Bones of hindlimbs are for walking and perching.

III. Bones of forelimbs are modified as wings.

IV. Shoulder bones are strong.

V. Breast bones hold flight muscles and are used to move wings up and down.

Which of the above statement(s) is/are correct?

Codes

a Only V   b III, IV and V

c I, III, IV and V   d I, II, III, IV and V

22. There are two snakes. We say snake A moves faster than B. Which of the following options, do you think correctly justify the statement?

a Snake A has light weight bones than snake B.

b Snake A forms large no. of loops than snake B.

c Snake A has strong bones than snake B.

d a, b and c all together justify the statement correct.

23.

I. Horse   –   Walking

II. Kangaroo   –   Slithering

III. Snail   –   Creeping

IV. Cockroach –   flying

V. Fish   –   Swimming

Which of the above combination is incorrect?

a Only II   b II and III

c III and IV   d Only IV

24. Observe the skeleton system given below. It shows some similarly looking joints with highlighted labelling. Identify A, B, C and D correctly with the help of the given options.

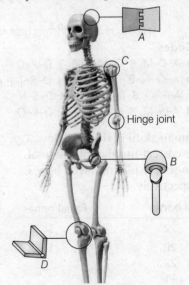

Hinge joint

Codes

	A	B	C	D
a	Fixed joint	Ball and socket	Ball and socket	Hinge joint
b	Hinge joint	Pivot	Ball and socket	Fixed joint
c	Ball and socket	Pivot	Ball and socket	Hinge joint
d	Pivot	Hinge joint	Ball and socket	Ball and socket

Codes

	P	Q	R	S
a	Swimmer	Knee bending	Top of the neck	Wrist movement
b	Sleeping straight	Sitting	Biceps	Ankle movement
c	Ankle movement	Wrist	Biceps	Knee bending
d	Top of neck	Swimming	Wrist movement	Ankle movement

25. While studying in classroom, teacher showed two figures *A* and *B* to students. She told that *A* is similar to *B* in working. According to you, what does *A* shows?

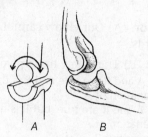

A   *B*

a Hinge movement
b Pivot
c Both a and b
d Ball and socket

26. Animals have different adaptations that enable them body movements. Given below is a list of some adaptations. Read them carefully and choose the option that shows the correct adaptation of respective animal.

I. Forelimbs modified into wings – Birds
II. Moves with 4 legs – Cockroach
III. Circular and longitudinal muscles – Earthworm.
IV. Two large disc shaped muscular foot – Snail

Codes

a I and II
b II and IV
c I and III
d I, II, III and IV

27.

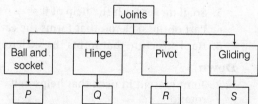

Analyse the above flow chart and identify *P, Q, R* and *S* (on the basis of example or its presence)

28. There is a table given below. Observe it carefully and identify the incorrect pair.

	Part of the skeleton	Organ(s) protected
A.	Cranium	Brain and eyes
B.	Ribs	Heart and lungs
C.	Vertebrae	Spinal cord
D.	Pelvis	Urinary bladder and kidney
E.	Collar bone	Shoulder

Codes

a Only B   b Only D
c Only A   d All are correct

29. When you touch your ear as shown in the given figure, you feel it soft but not hard. What do you think it has?

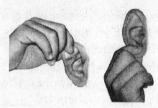

a It has soft bone
b It has cartilage, not bone
c It has tendon and cartilage
d It has ligament only

30. The vertebrae are hollow at the centre and are joined together to form a tube-like structure, through which the spinal cord runs. Then, out of the 33 vertebrae, How many are present in the following

I. In the neck or down to the upper chest.
II. Vertebrae extended to the back.
III. The lower back between the hips and chest.

Codes

	I	II	III		I	II	III
a	5	7	12	b	12	7	5
c	7	12	5	d	12	5	7

31. In a cricket match, when a bowler swings his hand to throw ball which of the following joint of his arm is working?

Choose a joint of the same type from list below:

	Joint		
A.	Pivot	1.	Knee
B.	Hinge	2.	Skull joints
C.	Gliding	3.	Head and neck
D.	Ball and socket	4.	Hip

Choose the correct option.

a A–1   b B–3   c C–2   d D–4

32. Observe the earthworm on soil in a garden (given in the figure alongside). You can see its body is made up of many rings joined end

to end. It has muscles but not bones. Which of the following is used by earthworm to move from one place to another?

Codes
a Simultaneous extension and grip
b Alternate extension, contraction and grip
c Contraction and grip
d Contraction and relaxation

33. Read the following passage and complete it with the help of an option that fills the missing links correctly.

_____ long bones form the palm. The wrist consists of _____ small bones. The fingers are made of phalanges. There are _____ bones in each finger but the thumb has only _____ bones.

Codes
a 5, 7, 2, 1   b 5, 8, 3, 2
c 5, 7, 4, 1   d 5, 8, 4, 3

34. Which of the following statement(s) is/are incorrect?

I. The contraction of the muscle pulls the bones during movement.

II. Mandible bone forms the lower jaw. It is the only skull bone that is movable.

III. Ball and socket joint is an example of joint found in hip and shoulder.

IV. The forearm has two bones.

V. Pelvic bones enclose the portion of our body above the stomach.

Codes
a I, II and V   b III and IV   c Only V   d IV and V

35. Consider the statements given below and opt the option that correctly declares them as true (T) or false (F).

I. All our bones are connected. The place where they meet are called joints.

II. Snails move with the help of a lubricant.

III. The body of cockroach has a hard covering forming an outer skeleton.

IV. The cartilages are harder than bones.

V. The movement and locomotion of all animals is exactly the same.

Codes

	I	II	III	IV	V			I	II	III	IV	V
a	T	F	T	T	T		b	T	T	F	T	T
c	T	T	F	T	T		d	T	F	T	F	F

36. Assertion (A) Our elbow cannot move backwards.

Reason (R) The elbow has a pivot joint.

a Both A and R are true and R is the correct explanation of A
b Both A and R are true, but R is not the correct explanation of A
c A is true, but R is fasle
d Both A and R are fasle

37. Solve the crossword with the help of given clues

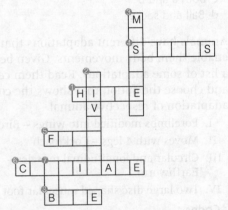

Across
1. A joint found in ankle, elbow and knees.
4. Smallest bone found in human body.
5. Snail moves with the help of it.
6. Part of the skeleton that forms the earlobe
8. Hard structure that forms the skeleton.

Down
2. Joint present in neck that helps in it rotation.
3. Help in the movement of body contraction and relaxation.
7. Bones that join with chest bone at one en and to the backbone at the other end.

Chapter 7

The Living Organisms and Their Surroundings

1. Adaptation is a characteristic that helps, an organism to survive in its environment. Which of the following can be considered as an adaptation that will help an organism to survive in unfavourable conditions?
   - A. Hide from their predators or prey
   - B. Stop reproduction
   - C. Survive in low light
   - D. Disperse their seeds

   a A and B   b B and C   c C and D   d All of these

2. Here are some drawings of birds feet. Which bird would be most likely to be adapted for swimming? Choose the correct option.

   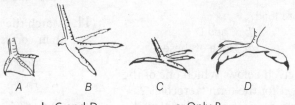

   A   *B*   *C*   *D*

   a A and D   b C and D   c Only B   d Only A

3. Which one of the following habitats have very cold weather and covered with snow throughout the year? Also, choose an adaptation of the animals of this region.

	Habitat		Adaptation
A.	Marine habitats	1.	Long hair
B.	Coastal habitats	2.	Fast and agile
C.	Grassland habitats	3.	Thick layer of fat
D.	Tundra habitats	4.	Streamlined body

   Codes
   a A – 1, 2   b B – 3, 4   c C – 2, 3   d D – 1, 3

4. Few organisms of different environment are given below. Which of the animals below is cold-blooded? Select the correct option.

   A   *B*   *C*   *D*

   a A and C   b Only B   c Only D   d A, B, C and D

5. Some of the plants are adapted to protect themselves from their predators, so that they could survive.

There are four plants shown below. Which of them show the best structural adaptation of leaves for protecting themselves from predators?

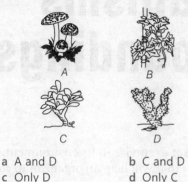

a A and D   b C and D
c Only D   d Only C

6. Camel is a desert animal. How does the camel survive in the heat during the day?

A. They go on mountains.

B. They stay in the burrows during the day.

C. They migrate to nearby forest during the day.

D. They eat more food.

a A and B   b C and D
c All of these   d None of these

7. A few terms are given below. Which one of the following is correct for the term 'xerocoles'? Also choose the appropriate examples of such animals from the list below.

	Term		Animal
A.	Animals which live in freshwater.	1.	Camel
B.	Animals which live in mountains.	2.	Mountain goat
C.	Animals which live in forest.	3.	Penguin
D.	Animals which live in desert.	4.	Whales

Codes

a A – 2   b B – 3
c C – 4   d D – 1

8. Our environment is made up of biotic and abiotic factors that interacts with each other. From the list given in the box below, categorise the factors as biotic/abiotic and choose the correct option.

1. Air	2. Plants	3. Bacteria
4. Fungi	5. Sunlight	6. Consumers
7. Temperature	8. Soil	

	Biotic	Abiotic
a	1, 2, 3, 4	5, 6, 7, 8
b	2, 3, 4, 6	1, 5, 7, 8
c	2, 3, 5, 7	1, 4, 6, 8
d	1, 5, 7, 8	2, 3, 4, 6

9. Few adaptations are given below. Which of them does not help organisms to protect themselves from predators?

A. Special body covering such as spines or hard shells.

B. Stings and bites that contain poison.

C. Strong feets to run fast.

D. Moving and feeding in groups to reduce the risk of any individual being caught by a predator.

a A and C   b B and C
c A, B and C   d A, B, C and D

10. Which of the following characteristics help(s) the water hyacinth to float on water?

A. Air spaces

B. Fleshy leaves

C. Waxy leaves

a Only A   b A and B
c A and C   d B and C

11. Match the organisms given in Column I with their corresponding adaptation in Column II.

	Column I		Column II
A.	Frog	1.	Hollow spongy bones
B.	Parrot	2.	Moist and slimy skin
C.	Bear	3.	Thick layer of fat under skin
D.	Seal	4.	Body covered with hairs
E.	Fish	5.	Eyes on side on head
F.	Rabbit	6.	Slippery scales

Codes

	A	B	C	D	E	F
a	1	2	3	4	5	6
b	6	4	5	3	2	1
c	2	1	4	3	6	5
d	2	1	6	5	4	3

12. Raheem is fond of animals. Thus, he always observe the animals and study about their habitats. Once, he came across an animal having a stream-lined and slippery body. What is the habitat of the animal?

a Water

b Desert

c Grassland

d Mountain

13. A form of adaptation of banyan tree is shown alongside. This adaptation is followed by the tree in its habitat. The roots help the tree to

Roots

A. absorb more sunlight.
B. get additional support.
C. take in H$_2$O nutrients from the soil.
D. absorb more water vapour from the air .

Codes

a	A and B	b	B and C
c	C and D	d	D and A

14. Animals use different parts of their bodies to move around. Which of the following rows shows an animal that is not correctly matched to its body parts for movement?

	Animal	Legs	Wings	Body	Flippers
a	Snake			✓	
b	Penguin		✓		
c	Cheetah	✓			
d	Dolphin				✓

15. Animals are characterised according to their habitat needs.

Some animals like the water spider and water beetle can stay underwater for a long time to hunt and feed because they___.

Water spider   Water beetle

a have air tubes for breathing
b have gills to breathe underwater
c can trap air with their body parts for breathing
d can breathe through their special nostrils

16. Which of the following statements correctly state(s) how some organisms react towards the amount of light in their environment?

A. Centipedes survive well in well-lit places.
B. Owls hunt well with the help of bright light.
C. Earthworms burrow into the soil to avoid sunlight.
D. Wild grass grows tall to increase its chances of survival.

Codes

a	Only C	b	C and D
c	A, C and D	d	A, B, C and D

17. What common adaptations do the water lettuce and water moss fern have to keep their leaves afloat?

A. They have fine hairs on their leaf surfaces.
B. They have waterproof leaves.
C. They have thick fleshy leaves.
D. They have leaves that can trap air bubbles.

Codes

a	A and B	b	B and C
c	A, B and C	d	B, C and D

18. Frogs have the ability to live on land and in water. Which of the adaptations enables them to do so?

A. They can trap air bubbles in their throat.
B. They have gills to help them breathe in water.
C. They have lungs to help them breathe when they are on land.
D. Their skin, when moist, can take in the air dissolved in the water.

Codes

a	A and B	b	B and C
c	C and D	d	A and D

19. Some inventions imitate the adaptations of animals. The diagram below shows a man snorkeling.

From which animal(s) did man get the idea of snorkeling gears and flippers?

A. Frog   B. Great diving beetle
C. Water stick insect   D. Tadpole

Codes

a	Only A	b	A and C
c	B and D	d	A, B and C

20. Which of the following animals is correctly matched to its structural adaptation?

	Animal	Adaptation
A.	Duck	webbed feet enable it to propel itself forward through the water
B.	Millipede	curls into a tiny ball when touched
C.	Polar bear	white fur enables it to be seen clearly in its habitat
D.	Fennec fox	large ears to keep itself warm

Codes

a	A and B	b	C and D
c	Only C	d	A, B and D

21. The animals shown below have adaptations which enable them to breathe in aquatic conditions.

Group A		Group B		
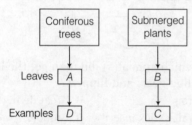				
Aquatic insects		Terrestrial insects		

The animals in Group A are different from those in Group B because they _____ .
   a can hold their breaths for long periods
   b breathe in dissolved oxygen from the water
   c take in oxygen from the water
   d trap air bubbles and carry their own supply of oxygen

22. The coconut is an excellent example of a water-dispersed fruit. Which of the following characteristics of the coconut fruit help(s) it to survive a long journey on water?
   A. The coconut fruit is big and light.
   B. The coconut fruit has a waterproof outer case.
   C. The coconut fruit has a fibrous husk containing numerous air spaces.

   a Only A   b Only C
   c A and C   d B and C

23.

Coniferous trees		Submerged plants
Leaves A		B
Examples D		C

Complete the flow chart above by choosing the appropriate option.

	A	B	C	D
a	Long thin	Waxy layer	Indian plum	Water hyacinth
b	Waxy layer	Spiny	*Acacia*	Firs
c	Needle shaped	Long thin	Pines	*Hydrilla*
d	Air cavities	Needle shaped	Cactus	Water lily

24. Flowering plants grow best in varying conditions. Different plants are suited to different conditions. The map shows the conditions in a garden that best suit some types of plants.

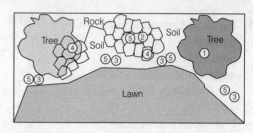

Which plant is best adapted to grow in the shade of a tree?
   a type 1   b type 2
   c type 3   d type 4

25. Plants are characterised by their habitats and adaptations to the environment for their survival. A few characteristic features of plants are given below:
   A. They lose a lot of water through transpiration.
   B. Their leaves are always broad and flat.
   C. They lose very little water through transpiration.
   D. Their roots grow very deep into the soil.

Which of the combination of above features are typical of desert plants?
   a A and B   b B and D
   c B and C   d C and D

26. If you happen to go to a desert, what changes do you expect to observe in the urine you excrete? You would
   A. excrete small amount of urine.
   B. excrete large amount of urine.
   C. excrete concentrated urine.
   D. excrete very dilute urine.

Which of the above would hold true?
   a A and C   b B and D
   c A and D   d A and B

27. Desert animals acquire some adaptations which help them to survive in the difficult conditions of desert.

Which of the following adaptations enable the camel to live in the desert?
   A. The hump(s) store(s) water to help it survive for long periods.
   B. The long eye lashes protect the eyes from the sand.
   C. The thick fur keeps it warm at night.
   D. The leathery skin on the knees protects it from getting burnt when it kneels on the sand.

Select the correct option.
   a A and B   b B, C and D
   c C and D   d A, B, C and D

28. Aquatic animals are able to survive in water just because they adopt various characteristics for the survival.

Which statements are true about the adaptations for movement in water for a dolphin and a typical fish? Select the correct option.

   A. Each has a streamlined body shape.

   B. Each has a tail to propel itself forward in the water.

   C. Each has a swim bladder to keep it afloat in water.

   D. Each has a pair of flippers to keep its balance in water.

Codes

a A and B   **b** A and D

c B and C   **d** C and D

29. How are penguins adapted to stay underwater for a long period of time?

   A. They can fast up to 100 days.

   B. They have webbed feet and flippers.

   C. Their heart rate increases to more than 100 beats per minute.

   D. Their muscles are able to store large amounts of oxygen.

Select the correct option from the above given statements.

   a A and B

   b B and C

   c Only D

   d A, B, C and D

30. Study the table carefully.

Type of beak	A	B	C	D
Example of bird				
Function	To scoop fish out of the water	To peck the ground for insects	To draw nectar from flowers	To crush hard seeds and nuts

Birds have different types of beaks to help them survive in the environment. Which beak(s) has/have been correctly matched to its/their function(s)?

   a Only A

   b A and C

   c B and D

   d B, C and D

31. The pie chart shows the time taken (in days) for a frog and a mosquito to develop from an egg to an adult.

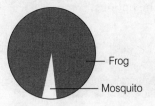

Assuming they have a similar rate of reproduction, which of the following statements are true?

   A. Within a given time frame, there will be more adult mosquitoes than adult frogs.

   B. From the pie chart, we can tell that there is a balanced food relationship between the frog and the mosquito.

   C. Rearing frogs to get rid of mosquitoes is not effective.

Codes

a A and B   **b** A and C

c B and C   **d** A, B and C

32. Consider the given figure carefully, which is showing the habitats of aquatic plants. What would be the correct statement regarding the function of such aquatic plants?

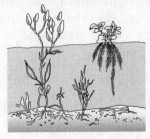

   A. Roots are much reduced in size and their main function is to hold the plant in place.

   B. Roots are long in size and hollow and their only function is to absorb nutrients.

   C. Roots does not play any important role in plant growth they only help plant to float on the surface of water.

   D. The stems are short and broad and just help in the transportation of water in the whole plant.

   E. Stems are long and narrow, with air spaces.

   F. Leaves are long and narrow in submerged plants.

Codes

a A, E and F   **b** B, C and D

c C and E   **d** C, D, E and F

33. Two different varieties of plants are given below. Observe them carefully. Select the habitat and adaptation in which they thrive from the options.

	Habitat	Adaptation
a	A. Terrestrial	A. Needle-like leaves
	B. Marine	B. Sloping branches
b	A. Hill regions	A. Cone-shaped
	B. Mountain regions	B. Leaves are needle-like
c	A. Mountain region	A. Cone-shaped and leaves are needle-like
	B. Desert region	B. Leaves are very small or spine-shaped
d	A. Terrestrial region	A. Cone-shaped and sloping branches
	B. Grassland regions	B. Long and hollow stems

34. Jafar want to investigate the breathing methods of the animals in a pond community. The figure below shows the different aquatic organisms living in the pond.

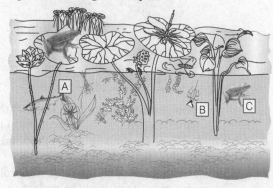

Which of the following rows shows the correct breathing methods of the aquatic animals, *A*, *B* and *C*?

	A	B	C
a	Breathing tube	Gills	Gills
b	Air bubbles	Air tube	Skin
c	Gills chambers	Breathing tube	Air tubes
d	Gills	Air tube	Lungs

35. Ali conducted a fair experiment to investigate the effect of temperature on two populations of plants. He then presented the results in the graph shown below.

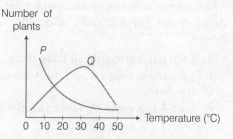

Based on the graph, which one of his observations below is correct?

a Plant *P* thrives best at 18°C.

b Plant *Q* can grow well in Indian climate.

c Plant *P* is likely to be a plant found in the desert.

d The growth of the population of plant *Q* depended on the population of plant *P*.

36. Ayushi kept three tanks of guppies, (Rainbow fishes) *P*, *Q* and *R*, with different combinations of food sources, preys and predators. The number of live guppies was counted over a period of 5 days and recorded as shown below.

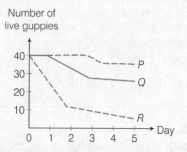

Which of the following conclusions made by Ayushi is/are correct?

A. Tank *P* is least suitable for the guppies.

B. Tank *R* has the most predators of guppies.

C. Tank *P* has more food sources than predators of the guppies.

D. Tank *Q* is suitable for the positive growth of guppy population.

a Only B

b A and B

c B and C

d B, C and D

37. Grizzly bears are well-adapted to the seasonal changes of a temperate forest.

How has the grizzly bear adapted itself to spend the winter season? Choose a structural adaptation and one behavioural adaptation of the grizzly bear.

	Structural adaptation		Behavioural adaptation
A.	It has thick layer of fat to keep it warm	1.	They do not possess any behavioural adaptation
B.	White colour of skin to reflect the cooling	2.	They keep warm by the heat produced during snow fall.
C.	The slippy fur present on the skin does not allow to freeze the ice on the body.	3.	They dig deep holes below the ice covered area.
D.	They already have the capability to prevent them from winter season.	4.	Grizzly bear hibernates during the winter.

Codes

a A – 4   b B – 3
c C – 1   d D – 2

38. Solve the crossword with the help of given clues.

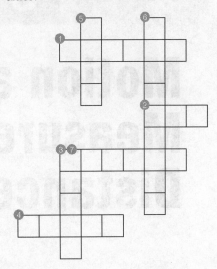

Across

1. Possess streamlined body shape
2. Tree adapted for very cold habitat, on Himalaya.
3. A desert plant, possess spike-shaped leaves.
4. Plants reproduce through _____ .

Down

5. Cone-shaped, needle-shaped leaves.
6. Living beings _____ their own kind.
7. A desert animal, adapted to store about 100 L of water in his hump.

Chapter 8

Motion and Measurement of Distance

A Motion and Its Types

1. Gagan Narang, who is among the India's best shooter shoots a bullet in a straight line on the wall. Which kind of motion did the bullet perform?

    I. Rectilinear   II. Circular   III. Rotational   IV. Curvilinear

Codes

  a I and II   **b** II and IV   **c** I and III   **d** III and IV

2. While playing a guitar, the guitarist plucks the string of his guitar. Which kind of motion does the plucked string undergo?

    I. Rectilinear   II. Periodic   III. Translatory   IV. Rotatory

Codes

  a I and II   **b** Only II   **c** II and III   **d** Only IV

3. A communication satellite is stationed in an orbit which is high above the earth. Which of the following type of motion will not be exhibited by it?

    I. Rotational motion   II. Rectilinear motion   III. Periodic motion   IV. Circular motion

Codes

  a I and III   **b** II and III   **c** I and II   **d** II and IV

4. Raju, who is a carpenter is boring holes in wooden planks using a drill machine. Which type of motion did the drill machine describe?

  a circular and oscillatory motion   **b** Rotatory and rectilinear motion

  c Rotatory and circular motion   **d** Rotatory and oscillatory motion

5. Complete the following passage using the suitable words given in the options below:

Rest and _____ are relative terms. An object may appear to be at _____ with respect to one object or in motion with respect to another _____. A passenger in a _____ train is at rest with respect to his _____, but is in motion with respect to an _____ standing at the platform.

Codes

  a rest, object, observer, moving, motion co-passengers
  b motion, rest, object, moving, co-passengers, observer
  c rest, motion, object, moving, observer, co-passengers
  d motion, rest, moving, object, observer, co-passengers

6. Consider the following statements and choose the incorrect one.

    I. Earth has three types of motion at the same time. These are circular, periodic and rotational motion.

    II. The motion of a swing is rectilinear as well as circular.

    III. A bicycle moving on a straight road has both rotational as well as rectilinear motion.

Codes

a Only I   b Only II
c Only III   d All are incorrect

7. Consider the following statements and choose the correct one.

    I. In a watch, only second hand exhibits periodic motion.

    II. Circular motion is the one in which an object as a whole travels along a circular path.

    III. In rotational motion, object not only spins on its axis but travels along a circular path too.

Codes

a Only I   b Only II
c Only III   d All are correct

8. Observe the following objects shown in the figure below. Which of them shows combination of one or more types of motion, simultaneously.

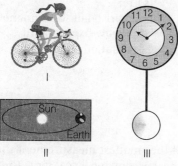

a I and II   b I and III
c II and III   d All of them

9. Fill in the blanks using the suitable words given in the box below:

(i) Distance	(ii) motion
(iii) periodic	(iv) measurement
(v) rotations	(vi) rectilinear
(vii) rotational	(viii) movement
(ix) circular	(x) circle

    I. The change in position of an object with time is called _____.

    II. A falling stone exhibits _____ motion.

    III. Motion of an object or a part of it around a fixed point is known as _____ motion.

    IV. A body repeating its motion after certain time interval is in _____ motion.

    V. Earth exhibits _____ motion around its own axis.

Codes

	I	II	III	IV	V
a	(iv)	(ix)	(iii)	(vi)	(v)
b	(ii)	(vi)	(ix)	(iii)	(vii)
c	(iv)	(v)	(iii)	(ix)	(vi)
d	(i)	(iii)	(vi)	(vii)	(ix)

10. State True (T) or False (F) statements.

    I. Motion of a swing is an example of rectilinear motion.

    II. A train moving on a curved track is said to be in random motion.

    III. Periodic motion repeats its motion after a fixed time interval.

    IV. The act of moving from one place to another is termed as movement.

    V. A butterfly flying in a garden is said to be in random motion.

Codes

	I	II	III	IV	V
a	T	F	T	F	T
b	T	T	F	T	F
c	F	F	T	F	T
d	F	T	F	T	F

11. Matrix matching.

	Column I		Column II
1.	Rectilinear motion	A.	
2.	Circular motion	B.	
3.	Rotational motion	C.	
4.	Periodic motion	D.	

Codes

	A	B	C	D			A	B	C	D
a	4	1	3	2		b	4	3	1	2
c	2	3	1	4		d	2	1	3	4

12. Assertion (A) A passenger sitting in a moving car is at rest with respect to fellow passengers.

Reason (R) An object is said to be in motion if it changes its position with time with respect to surroundings.

Select the correct answer from the options given as below:

a Both A and R are true and R is the correct explanation of A

b Both A and R are true, but R is not the correct explanation of A

c A is true, but R is false

d A is false, but R is true

13. Assertion (A) A moving merry-go-round shows both rotational as well as circular motion.

Reason (R) In circular motion, an object as a whole travels along a circular path but in rotational motion, the object spins on its axis.

Select the correct answer from the codes given below:

Codes

a Both A and R are true and R is the correct explanation of A

b Both A and R are true but R is not the correct explanation of A

c A is true but R is false

d A is false but R is true

14. Solve the following crossword using hints given below.

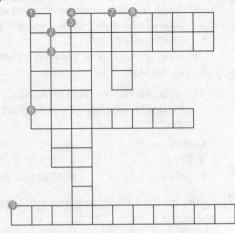

Across

2. Motion which repeats itself after some time interval …

4. SI unit of length …

6. Motion of earth around the sun in its orbit …

8. The object which does not change its position with respect to time and surroundings is said to be in …

9. Motion in a straight line …

Down

1. This invention made the greatest change in mode of transport … .

3. When the object changes its position with respect to time and surrounding it is in … .

5. Comparison of some unknown quantity with some fixed quantity … .

7. The duration of happening of an event …

B Measurement

1. Consider the figure shown as below. What should be the most appropriate position of the eye of an observer in order to measure the length accurately?

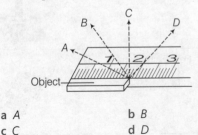

a A

b B

c C

d D

2. If the smallest measurement that can be measured using a scale is 0.1 mm, then the length of 1 m in the scale is divided into how many equal parts?

a 1000   b 5000

c 10000   d 100

3. Rohan travelled by car to Mumbai. He travelled 292 km in first 3 h, then he started driving his car faster and travelled 400 km in next 4 h. How far did he travelled in 7 h?

a 108 km   b 692 km

c 984 km   d 1184 km

4. Ananya wants to measure the length and breadth of her classroom using her foot as a unit of length. If the length of her foot is 30 cm and she covers 20 foot steps while covering length of classroom and 15 foot steps while covering breadth of classroom. What will be the length and breadth of her classroom in cms?

	Length	Breadth
a	450	600
b	600	450
c	500	400
d	400	500

5. A pile of some identical five rupee coins are placed over a metre scale as shown in the figure below.

The thickness of five rupee coin is

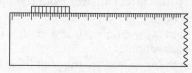

a 2 mm
b 3 mm
c 2 cm
d 3 cm

6. You are provided three scales A, B and C as shown in figure. To measure a length of 10 cm which of them can be used?

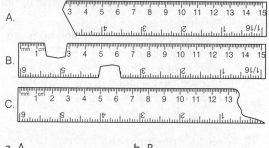

a A
b B
c C
d All of these

7. Figure shows a measuring scale which is usually supplied with a geometry box. Which of the following distance cannot be measured with this scale by using it only once?

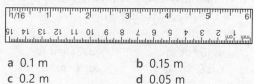

a 0.1 m
b 0.15 m
c 0.2 m
d 0.05 m

8. Four pieces of wooden sticks A, B, C and D are placed along the length of 30 cm long scale as shown in figure. Which one of them is 3.4 cm in length?

a A
b B
c C
d D

9. Geeta's teacher asked her to measure the total length of given figure. What will Geeta require for this purpose?

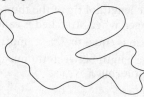

a A thread
b A scale
c Both 'a' and 'b'
d Neither 'a' nor 'b'

10. A person needs to measure his micro SD card but the scale he has is broken. What will be the length of his micro SD card if he measures it as shown in figure given below in mm.

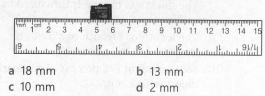

a 18 mm
b 13 mm
c 10 mm
d 2 mm

11. Consider the following statements and choose the incorrect statement.

I. Measurement of distance actually refers to measurement of lengths.

II. A measurement is complete even without a number and consisting a unit only.

II. SI units is the short form of "Systeme International d 'Unites'".

Codes
a I and II
b Only II
c II and III
d All of these

12. Consider the following statements and choose the correct statement.

I. SI unit of length is metre.

II. A scale or a measuring tape both can be used if the object to be measured is straight.

III. The length of a curved line can be measured using a thread and a scale.

Codes
a I and II
b II and III
c I and IV
d All of these

13. Fill in the blanks using the words given in box below.

(i) 1000		(ii) hand span	
(iii) distance		(iv) foot	
(v) 1000000		(vi) measurement	
(vii) 1 cm		(viii) unit	
(ix) cubit			

    I. Every measurement consists of a number and a ....

    II. The length of forearm from elbow to fingertips is called ....

    III. The length of tip of the thumb and little finger, when stretched is called ....

    IV. 1 km is equal to .... mm.

    V. The length between thumb and heel of the foot is called ....

Codes

	I	II	III	IV	V
a	viii	ix	ii	v	iv
b	iv	iii	ii	i	ix
c	viii	ii	v	iv	ix
d	iv	iii	ix	i	iv

14. State True or False.

    I. The thickness of wire is measured in millimetres.

    II. The length or breadth of a room is measured in kilometres.

    III. Measurement is a process of comparing an object with a unit.

    IV. The length of the space between two places is called measurement.

    V. The SI unit of length is kilometre.

Codes

	I	II	III	IV	V
a	F	T	F	T	T
b	T	F	T	F	F
c	T	T	F	T	F
d	F	T	T	T	F

15. Matrix matching.

	Column I		Column II
A.	Cubit	1.	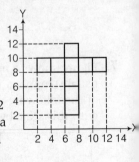
B.	hand-span	2.	
C.	pace	3.	
D.	foot	4.	

Codes

	A	B	C	D		A	B	C	D
a	4	1	3	2	b	3	1	2	4
c	1	3	4	2	d	3	1	4	2

16. Assertion (A) Elastic measuring tapes cannot be used to measure lengths.

Reason (R) Elastic objects are the one which can stretch easily even when small force is applied.

Select the correct answer from the options given below:

    a Both (A) and (R) are true and (R) is the correct explanation of (A).

    b Both (A) and (R) are true, but (R) is not the correct explanation of (A).

    c (A) is true, but (R) is false.

    d (A) is false, but (R) is true.

17. Assertion (A) The length of a curved line can be measured by using a thread and a scale.

Reason (R) A measuring tape is used to measure the length of a curved line.

Select the correct answer from the options given below.

    a Both (A) and (R) are true and (R) is the correct explanation of (A).

    b Both (A) and (R) are true, but (R) is not the correct explanation of (A).

    c (A) is true, but (R) is false.

    d (A) is false, but (R) is true.

18. Consider the following graph which is used to measure the area of paper cutting placed in it. The X and Y axes represent the length of 2 cm per division. The area of the paper cutting will be

    a 18 cm sq   b 24 cm sq

    c 36 cm sq   d 9 cm sq

Chapter 9

Light: Shadows and Reflections

A Light

1. Four students A, B, C and D looked through pipes of different shapes to see a candle flame as shown in figure below.

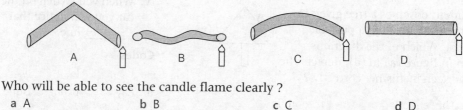

   Who will be able to see the candle flame clearly ?
   a A   b B   c C   d D

2. When a person passes under a leafy tree during a sunny day, he observes some bright circular patches of light on the ground under the tree. These patches are
   a shadows of sun   b images of sun
   c pinhole images of sun   d sun

3. Geeta has three materials P, Q and R such that when she tries to see through P she can see everything faintly, while through Q she cannot see anything and through R she can see everything clearly. P, Q and R are respectively
   a Transparent, translucent, opaque   b Opaque, translucent, transparent
   c Translucent, opaque, transparent   d Opaque, transparent, translucent

4. A pinhole camera is based on the principle that light propagates in a straight line. Which of the following figures correctly depicts the image formation by pinhole camera ?

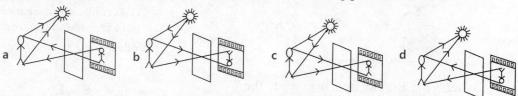

5. What could be the reason for the objects being visible even if sunlight is not allowed to enter the room ?
   a Objects are able to store light and reflect back in the absence of sunlight.
   b Air around the objects allows the scattered light to pass through it to make objects visible.
   c Objects themselves scatter the light so as to make themselves visible.
   d None of the above

6. In a school activity, Rohit and Geeta has been asked to arrange some given objects based on their transparency. The objects are as follows.

> Wall, book, frosted glass, aquarium, mirror, sunglasses, corrective glasses, bulb.

Who has made the correct arrangement ?

	Rohit	Geeta
Transparent	Corrective glasses, bulb, aquarium	Corrective glass, bulb, aquarium, mirror
Translucent	Frosted glass, sunglasses	Sunglasses
Opaque	Wall, book, mirror	Wall, book, frosted glass

- a Rohit
- b Geeta
- c Both Rohit and Geeta
- d Neither Rohit nor Geeta

7. A student observes a tree given in figure below through a pin hole camera. Which of the diagrams given in figure (a) to (d), depicts the image seen by his/her correctly ?

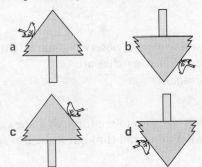

8. A girl is holding a mirror 15 cm in front of herself to see a bird that is 100 cm behind her.

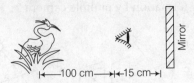

What is the distance from her eyes to the image of the bird ?

- a 215 cm
- b 100 cm
- c 115 cm
- d 130 cm

9. Consider the following statements and choose the correct one(s).

I. We cannot see behind a wall due to rectilinear propagation of light.

II. A pinhole camera works on the principle of rectilinear propagation of light.

III. Images formed by a pinhole camera are always real and inverted.

Codes

a Only I	b Only II
c Only III	d All of these

10. Fill in the blanks using suitable words using the suitable option given below.

I. _____ is a form of energy. It gives energy to plants to prepare their food.

II. A _____ is a narrow path of light which is represented by arrowhead.

III. A _____ consists of many rays which are generally parallel to each other.

IV. When you switch on the headlights of your car you will notice that rays travel in _____ line.

Codes

	I	II	III	IV
a	Ray	Beam	Light	Straight
b	Light	Beam	Ray	Straight
c	Light	Ray	Beam	Straight
d	Straight	Beam	Ray	Light

11. State true or false using codes given below.

I. Electric bulb being man-made source of light is considered non-luminous object.

II. Transparent objects appear to be transparent because they reflect all the light strikes on its surface.

III. Opaque objects reflect or absorb all the light incident on it.

IV. Rectilinear propagation of light enables us to see around the corners.

Codes

	I	II	III	IV
a	F	T	F	T
b	T	F	T	T
c	T	T	F	T
d	T	F	T	F

12. Assertion (A) Non-luminous objects cannot be visualised without the existence of luminous objects.

Reason (R) We can discriminate between objects when they reflect light incident on them.

Select the correct answer from the options given below

a Both A and R are true and R is the correct explanation of A.

b Both A and R are true but R is not the correct explanation of A.

c A is true, but R is false.

d A is false, but R is true.

13. Assertion (A) The window panes are generally made of transparent glass.

Reason (R) The transparent objects do not allow all the light to pass through them.

Select the correct answer from the options given below

a Both A and R are true and R is the correct explanation of A.

b Both A and R are true, but R is not the correct explanation of A.

c A is true, but R is false.

d A is false, but R is true.

14. Matrix matching

Column I		Column II	
A.	Torch	1.	Luminous
B.	Mirror	2.	Transparent
C.	Moon	3.	Translucent
D.	Clear water	4.	Opaque
E.	Cellophane sheet	5.	Non-luminous

Codes

	A	B	C	D	E
a	1	2	3	4	5
b	5	4	1	2	3
c	1	4	5	2	3
d	1	3	5	2	4

Direction (Q. Nos. 15 and 16)

Read the following information and answer the questions that follow :

Luminous bodies like the sun, a gas flame and an electric light filament are visible since they are light sources. The objects other than luminous objects are visible only when they are in the presence of light from the luminous objects.

15. In the figure given below, a kid is watching TV at his home. How many luminous objects are there ?

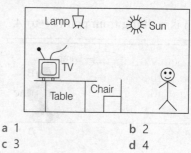

a 1   b 2
c 3   d 4

16. Pick the odd one out.

a Boy
b Chair
c Television
d Table

B) Shadow

1. Which of the following is/are not always necessary to observe a shadow ?

I. Sun   II. Screen

III. Source of light   IV. Opaque object

Codes

a Only I   b I and III
c II and IV   d Only III

2. Shadow give us some information about the shape of the object. Which of the following can never form a circular shadow ?

a A ball   b A flat disc
c A shoe box   d An ice-cream cone

3. Shivani observed the shadow of a tree at 8:00 a.m., 12:00 noon and 3:00 p.m. Which of the following statements is closest to her observation about the shape and size of the shadow ?

a The shape of the shadow of the tree changes but the size remains the same.

b The size of the shadow of the tree changes but the shape remains the same.

c Both the size and shape of the shadow of the tree change.

d Neither the shape nor the size of the shadow changes.

4. A frosted glass and a wooden cone are placed in line with each other. A torch is shone directly at both the objects and their shadows were cast onto the screen.

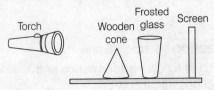

Which one of the following shadows would be seen on the screen ?

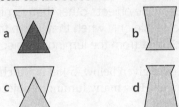

5. Rohan is walking from points *D* to *A*.

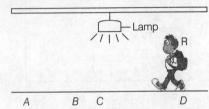

When he walks from point *D* to point *A*, which one of the following shows the correct order of the length of his shadows from the longest to the shortest ?

a *A, B, D, C*   b *D, A, B, C*
c *C, B, A, D*   d *A, D, B, C*

6. The size and shape of the shadow change with time. Which of the following figure depicts that the girl is standing in afternoon time?

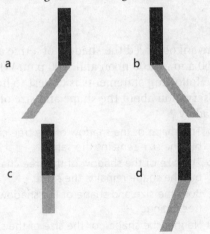

7. Consider the following figure in which two kids are playing with a torch.

Which of the following statements are correct with respect to the shadow formation.

I. The shadow is formed when an opaque object is placed in the path of light.
II. Shadow is formed as light rays cannot bend.
III. Shadow is formed when it reflects light into our eyes.

Codes
a I and II   b II and III
c I and III   d All are correct

8. In which of the following figures shown below shadow is formed.

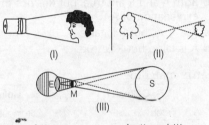

a I and II   b II and III
c I and III   d All of these

9. Consider the following statements and choose the incorrect one:

I. Our shadows are longer in the morning than at noon.
II. The incident angle is larger in the morning which makes the shadows longer.
III. Light is incident normally at noon due to which the size of shadow is reduced.

Codes
a Only I   b Only II
c Only III   d All of these

10. Fill in the blanks using suitable option given below

I. Eclipses are fundamental examples of _____.
II. A _____ is needed to form a shadow.
III. Shadows are the _____ but _____ images of an object.
IV. The size of a shadow varies with the inclination of _____.

Codes

	I	II	III	IV
a	Shadows	screen	real, dark	source
b	Shadows	screen	dark, real	source
c	Real	shadows	dark, source	screen
d	Source	screen	dark, real	shadows

11. State true or false using codes given below.

    I. The shape of a shadow is same as the shape of object because light passes through the object to form the shadow.

    II. One of the shadow of flying bird is also formed on sky which acts as a screen.

    III. Shadow of an object is always erect.

    IV. A shadow in a dark room always appears on the opposite side of object.

Codes

	I	II	III	IV
a	T	F	T	F
b	F	T	F	T
c	F	F	F	T
d	F	F	T	F

12. Assertion (A) Shadows are formed on the same side of the source of light.

Reason (R) Shadow of an object is cast only when a translucent object obstructs the path of light incident on it from its back side.

Select the correct answer from the options given below :

    a Both A and R are true and R is the correct explanation of A.

    b Both A and R are true, but R is not the correct explanation of A.

    c A is true, but R is false.

    d Both A and R are false.

13. Assertion (A) Shadows formed using fluorescent tube light are much sharper and clear than that of candle or electric bulb.

Reason (R) An electric bulb and candle are quite small sources of light than a fluorescent tube light due to which most of the light is obstructed by the object and shadow becomes much clearer.

Select the correct answer from the options given below:

    a Both A and R are true and R is the correct explanation of A

    b Both A and R are true, but R is not the correct explanation of A.

    c A is true, but R is false.

    d A is false, but R is true.

14. Matrix-matching

	Column A		Column
I.	At noon	p.	Lighter part of shadow
II.	In the morning	q.	Darker part of shadow
III.	Dark object	r.	Smaller than object
IV.	Umbra	s.	Larger than object
V.	Penumbra	t.	No shadow

Codes

	I	II	III	IV	V
a	p	r	q	t	s
b	r	s	t	q	p
c	s	r	t	p	q
d	t	s	r	q	p

✎ Direction (Q.Nos 15 and 16)

Read the following information and answer the questions that follow:

A shadow is formed where light is missing. A dark shadow i.e. umbra is formed where no light falls and a light shadow i.e. penumbra is formed where some light falls, but some is blocked. If the light source is very tiny and concentrated in one place only a sharp shadow is formed.

15. Identify the X and Y in the given figure.

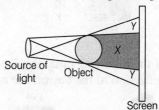

    a X - umbra, Y - penumbra

    b X - penumbra, Y - umbra

    c X - penumbra, Y - penumbra

    d X - umbra, Y - umbra

16. The shape and size of a shadow depends on

    a position of source of light

    b shape and size of object

    c distance between object and source of light

    d All of the above

C Reflection of Light

1. Two students while sitting across a table looked down onto its top surface. They noticed that they could see their own and each other's image. The table top is likely to be made of
   a unpolished wood
   b red stone
   c polished wood
   d wood top covered with cloth

2. Geeta had some red liquid in a beaker. She added some yellow colour to it. Then she looked into the beaker using a torch as shown in the figure.

What would be the colour of the image of the beaker on the screen?

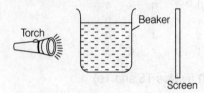

   a Red
   b Orange
   c Yellow
   d Black

3. A boy looks into the mirror as shown below.

Boy

Which of the following options shows the correct reflection of the boy on the mirror?

a
b
c
d

4. Observe the given picture figure carefully.

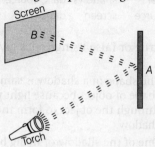

A patch of light is obtained at *B*, when the torch is lighted as shown. Which of the following is kept at position *A* to get this patch of light?
   a A wooden board
   b A glass sheet
   c A sheet of white paper
   d A mirror

5. A periscope can be used to spot objects which are not placed in our direct view. Which of the diagrams shows the light path in a periscope correctly?

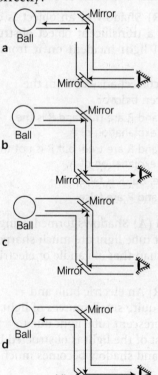

a
b
c
d

6. Consider the following statements and choose the incorrect ones.

    I. Reflection can be observed both in case of opaque as well as translucent objects.

    II. Images formed by reflection are always virtual.

    III. Images formed on standing water are laterally inverted.

Codes

  a Only I

  b Only II

  c Only III

  d All of the above

7. Fill in the blanks using suitable words using the suitable option given below :

    I. _____ is possible only using shining or polished surface.

    II. Images formed by plane mirror are actually _____ the mirror but appears _____ it.

    III. _____ can produce both real as well as virtual images.

    IV. A _____ works on reflection of light from two plane mirrors arranged parallel to each other.

Codes

	I	II	III	IV
a	Reflection	in front of, behind	periscope	lateral inversion
b	Lateral inversion	in front of, behind	periscope	reflection
c	Periscope	behind, in front of	lateral inversion	reflection
d	Lateral inversion	behind, in front of	reflection	periscope

8. State true or false using codes given below:

    I. Regular reflection from rough surfaces causes glare in our eyes.

    II. Images formed on cinema screen are real images.

    III. Glass helps to change the direction of light that falls on it.

    IV. The reflection phenomena suggest that light do not travel in straight line.

Codes

	I	II	III	IV
a	F	T	F	F
b	T	F	F	F
c	F	T	T	T
d	T	T	F	F

9. **Assertion** (A) Reflection is caused by only opaque objects like plane mirror.

Reason (R) Black surface do not reflect any light incident on it.

Select the correct answer from the options given below.

  a Both A and R are true and R is the correct explanation of A

  b Both A and R are true, but R is not the correct explanation of A

  c A is true, but R is false

  d A is false, but R are true

10. **Assertion** (A) Images formed by a plane mirror is always virtual and erect.

Reason (R)

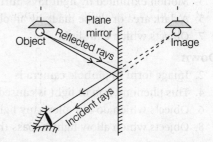

Select the correct answer from the options given below

  a Both A and R are true and R is the correct explanation of A

  b Both A and R are true, but R is not the correct explanation of A

  c A is true, but R is false

  d A is false, but R are true

11. Matrix-matching

	Column A		Column B
I.	Regular reflection	p.	Mirror
II.	Diffused reflection	q.	Glass
III.	No reflection	r.	Air
		s.	Wood
		t.	Metals
		u.	Paper

Codes

	I	II	III
a	p,u	r,s	q,t
b	q,t	r,s	p,u
c	q,r	s,u	p,t
d	p,t	s,u	q,r

Read the following information and answer the questions that follow

A plane mirror is a flat sheet of glass having silver coating on one of its side. This coating makes the plane mirror shiny and gives maximum reflection. The coating is protected by another coating of red paint.

12. Which type of reflection is caused by plane mirror?

    a Regular reflection   **b** Diffused reflection

    c Both regular as well as diffused reflection   **d** None of the above

13. Which among the following is not true regarding the image formation by plane mirror?

    a Image is formed behind the mirror   **b** Laterally inverted image is formed

    c Virtual and erect image is formed   **d** Virtual and inverted image is formed

14. Solve the crossword using hints given below

Across

    1. Butter paper is an example of _____ Object

    3. Motion exhibited by light rays during their propagation

    5. A dark area or shape made by an object by blocking rays of light

    7. Objects which emit light

Down

    2. Image form in pinhole camera is _____

    4. This phenomenon of light is caused by opaque surfaces

    6. Objects which do not allow any light to pass through them

    8. Objects which allow light to pass through them completely

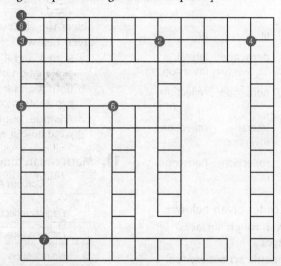

Chapter 10

Electricity and Circuit

 A **Electric Current and Circuit**

1. A circuit containing three bulbs in series connected to a battery of three cells is shown in diagram below.

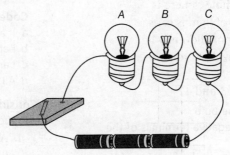

When the switch is moved to 'ON' position,
  a the bulb *A* will glow first
  c the bulb *C* will glow first

  b the bulb *B* will glow first
  d all bulbs will glow together

2. In which of the following circuits will the bulb or bulbs glow with most brightness?

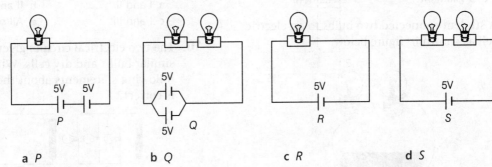

  a *P*
  b *Q*
  c *R*
  d *S*

3. Consider the following circuits and choose the option which shows the correct direction of current.

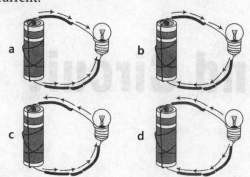

📝 **Direction** (Q. Nos. 4-5) Observe the diagram of an electric bulb shown below carefully and answer the questions that follow.

4. What is the function of 3 and 4?
- a Provide support to the bulb
- b Act as positive and negative terminals of the bulb
- c Act as source of energy to the filament of the bulb
- d All of the above

5. Which part of the bulb glows to produce light?
- a 2-Glass case
- b 1-Filament
- c 5-Filament
- d 2-Filament

6. A student connected two bulbs to an electric cell as shown in figure below.

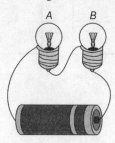

The bulbs did not glow. What could be the most suitable reason for the problem?
- a Filament of bulb A is broken
- b Filament of bulb B is broken
- c Filament of both the bulbs is broken
- d All of the above

7. Paheli have two bulbs, a cell and a switch to make an electrical circuit. Which of the following electrical circuit should not be set up?

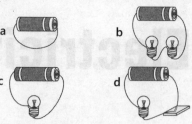

8. In which of the following diagrams the bulb will glow?

Codes
- a II and III
- b I and II
- c I and III
- d All of the above will glow

9. Consider the following statements and choose the incorrect statement.
- I. A switch helps us to use electricity as per our requirement.
- II. In closed position, a switch consists of an air gap between its terminals.
- III. A switch is the source of electric current in a circuit.

Codes
- a I and II
- b II and III
- c I and III
- d All of these

10. The two electrical circuits given here consist of similar bulbs and dry cells. Which of the following statements about the given circuits is correct?

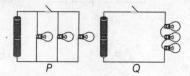

- a The bulbs in circuit Q are brighter than those in circuit P when all the switches are closed.
- b If the middle bulb in circuit Q blows, at least one bulb will still be able to light up.
- c All the bulbs in circuit P will not light up when the switch is open.
- d One bulb in circuit P will light up when the switch is open.

11. Fill the blanks using suitable words using the suitable option given below.

   I. An —— converts chemical energy into electrical energy.

   II. A bulb is said to be —— if its filament breaks.

   III. There are —— terminals in an electric cell.

   IV. An —— is a continuous path along which current flows.

Codes

	I	II	III	IV
a	Electric circuit	open	two	electric cell
b	Electric cell	fused	multiple	electric circuit
c	Electric cell	fused	two	electric circuit
d	Electric cell	open	multiple	electric circuit

12. State true or false using codes given below.

   I. A fuse is used to complete or break an electric circuit.

   II. Current in a cell flows from positive terminal to negative terminal.

   III. A circuit is said to be open if current flows through it.

   IV. A filament is a part of bulb which glows when current pass through it.

Codes

	I	II	III	IV			I	II	III	IV
a	T	T	F	T		b	F	T	T	F
c	F	F	F	T		d	F	T	F	T

13. Matrix matching.

I.	Ammeter	p.	—|⊦----|⊦—
II.	Voltmeter	q.	—o⁄o—
III.	Bulb	r.	—(A)—
IV.	Battery	s.	—(⊗)—
V.	Switch	t.	—(V)—

Codes

	I	II	III	IV	V
a	q	r	p	t	s
b	r	t	s	p	q
c	t	r	p	s	q
d	t	s	r	p	q

14. **Assertion** (A) Switch is a simple device which is used to make or break a circuit.

   Reason (R) An electric circuit is a complete and continuous path along which current flows.

Select the correct answer from the options given below

   a Both A and R are correct and R is the correct explanation of A

   b Both A and R are correct and R is not the correct explanation of A

   c A is true, but R is false

   d R is true, but A is false

15. **Assertion** (A) A bulb does not work if it is fused.

   Reason (R) A large amount of current passes through a fused bulb.

Select the correct answer from the options given below.

   a Both A and R are correct and R is the correct explanation of A

   b Both A and R are correct and R is not the correct explanation of A

   c A is true, but R is false

   d R is true, but A is false

16. In a school activity Geeta and Rohit were given a torch shown below to identify each part along with the function of each part. They recorded their observations in a table given below.

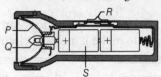

Geeta

Part		Function
P	Reflector	To reflect back light emitted by bulb
Q	Bulb	To produce light
R	Switch	To make or break a circuit
S	Battery	To produce electricity in a circuit

Rohit

Part		Function
P	Reflector	To protect the torch from short-circuit
Q	Bulb	To produce light
R	Sliding Switch	To make or break a circuit
S	Cell	To produce electricity in a circuit

Whose observations are correct?

   a Geeta

   b Rohit

   c Both Geeta and Rohit

   d Neither Geeta nor Rohit

B Electrical Conductivity and Domestic Circuits

1. Consider the diagram shown below. Using which of the following options the bulb will not glow if connected between A and B.

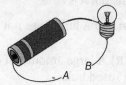

    a A steel spoon   b A metal clip
    c A plastic clip   d A copper wire

2. Saloni's teacher taught her that pencil lead is a good conductor of electricity. To observe its conducting nature she sets up a circuit shown below.

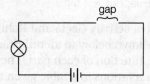

    Which of the following pencils can be placed in the gap to make it a closed circuit?

    a   b
    c   d

3. In an experiment a student placed the rods with four bells A, B, C and D which are in working order.

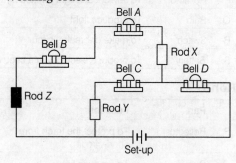

    Set-Up A

    The results of his experiment are given in the table below.

Set-up	Does it ring?
Bell A	Yes
Bell B	Yes
Bell C	No
Bell D	Yes

Which among the following options is the most suitable conclusion?

    a X and Y are insulators whereas Z is conductor
    b X and Y are conductors whereas Z is insulator
    c Y is an insulator alone
    d Y is a conductor alone

4. Geeta made a circuit card as shown below.

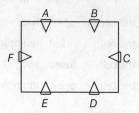

    The table shows the results when the different clips of the circuit card are connected.

Clips connected to circuit tester	Light bulb of circuit tester
A and C	Lights up
A and E	Lights up
B and C	Does not light up
B and F	Does not light up
D and E	Lights up
E and F	Lights up

The light bulb will not light up when clips ——— are connected.

    a A and F   b B and D
    c C and D   d C and E

5. Consider the circuit diagram shown below.

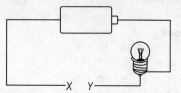

    Which one of the following should be placed between X and Y so as to complete the circuit.

    a A plastic ruler
    b A wooden block
    c An eraser
    d A piece of pencil lead

6. Paheli set up the following circuits to check if materials W, X, Y and Z were electrical conductors.

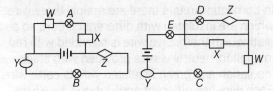

She recorded her observations in the table below.

Bulb	Did the bulb light up?
A	Yes
B	No
C	Yes
D	No
E	Yes

From the observations which materials are electrical conductors or electrical insulators?

	Electrical conductors	Electrical insulators
a	X	W, Y, Z
b	W, X, Y	Z
c	W, Z	X, Y
d	W, X	Y, Z

7. An electrician used the symbols shown on the right to draw a diagram of a circuit in which four lights and a fan are connected such that each operates independently.

Circuit symbols	
Ⓕ	Generator
Ⓖ	Fan
⊖	Light Bulb
⊠	Switch

Which of the following circuit diagrams did the electrician draw?

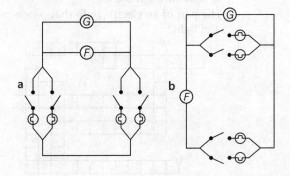

10. ...

11. Graphite ...
Insulator ...

8. Observe the circuit diagram shown below.

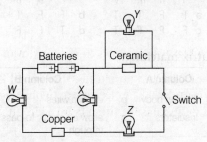

Which of the following statements are true when the switch is closed?

A. If bulb W blows, bulbs X, Y and Z will still light up.

B. If bulb X blows, bulbs W, Y and Z will still light up.

C. If bulb Y blows, bulbs W, X and Z will still light up.

D. If bulb Z blows, only bulbs W and X will still light up.

Codes

a A and D	b A and B
c B and D	d B, C and D

9. Fill the blanks using suitable words given in the options below:

I. .... allow electric current to pass through them.

II. .... is an example of insulator.

III. Thermocol being .... does not allow current to pass through it.

IV. Copper and .... are used to make electric wires.

Codes

	I	II	III	IV
a	Conductors	Water	Insulator	Aluminium
b	Aluminium	Insulator	Conductors	Water
c	Conductors	Aluminium	Water	Insulator
d	Insulator	Aluminium	Conductor	Water

10. State true or false using codes given below.

    I. Metal wires of an electric circuit can be replaced with jute string.

    II. Graphite being a non-metal is an insulator.

    III. Outer covering of electric wires are made up of plastic because it is a good conductor.

    IV. Air is an insulator.

Codes

	I	II	III	IV		I	II	III	IV
a	T	F	T	T	b	F	F	T	T
c	F	F	F	T	d	T	F	F	F

11. Matrix matching.

	Column A		Column B
I.	Human body	p.	electric wires
II.	Insulators	q.	allow electricity to pass through
III.	Conductors	r.	do not allow electricity to pass through
IV.	Copper	s.	conductor

Codes

	I	II	III	IV		I	II	III	IV
a	p	q	r	s	b	q	r	s	p
c	s	p	r	q	d	s	r	q	p

12. Assertion (A) Electricity can only flow if there is a complete circuit made of conductors.

Reason (R) Conductors are the materials which do not allow electric current to pass through them.

Select the correct answer from the options given below.

  a Both A and R are correct and R is the correct explanation of A

  b Both A and R are correct and R is not the correct explanation of A

  c A is true, but R is false

  d R is true, but A is false

13. Assertion (A) Electricians use rubber gloves while repairing an electric switch at home.

Reason (R) Some materials do not allow electric current to pass through them which are known as insulators.

Select the correct answer from the options given below.

  a Both A and R are correct and R is the correct explanation of A

  b Both A and R are correct and R is not the correct explanation of A

  c A is true, but R is false

  d R is true, but A is false

Direction (Q. Nos. 14-16)

Read the following information and answer the questions that follow

In domestic circuits there are mainly three wires which are insulated with different colours so as to distinguish them. Live wire is provided with red insulation, neutral wire is provided with black insulation and green insulated wire is earth wire. Each wire has different applications. Live wire provides the necessary current to the appliances whereas neutral wire is to carry away the current to the power house. Earth wire is used as a safety wire and connects the appliances to earth.

14. Which of the three wires in a domestic circuit is used as a safety wire?

  a Live wire   **b** Earth wire

  c Neutral wire   **d** None of these

15. Which of the three wires is used to take away the current back to the power house?

  a Live wire   **b** Earth wire

  c Neutral wire   **d** None of these

16. Domestic wiring is done by using copper wires and not silver wires though silver is the best conductor. Why is it so?

  a Copper is more ductile than silver

  b Copper is cheaper than silver

  c Copper is eco-friendly but silver is not

  d Copper is much in abundance than silver

17. Solve the following crossword using hints given below.

Across

  2. The ends of an electric circuit are known as

  4. It is required to run our appliances

  6. Electric current starts to flow from this end

  7. A device which is used to make or break a circuit

Down

  1. Arrangement which provides a complete path for electricity

  3. These materials do not allow electric current to flow through them

  5. The part of an electric bulb that produces heat and light

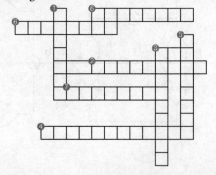

Chapter 11

Fun with Magnets

A Properties of a Magnet

1. Geeta broke a long bar magnet into two pieces as shown below.

Identify the poles of each piece.

	North	South
a	Y and P	X and Q
b	X and P	Y and Q
c	X and Q	Y and P
d	X and Y	P and Q

2. Consider the following diagrams.

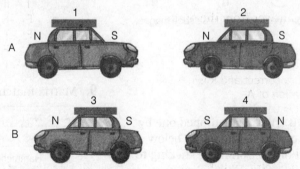

Based on above diagram which of the following statement is correct?
a In A, cars 1 and 2 will come closer and in B, cars 3 and 4 will come closer.
b In A, cars 1 and 2 will move away from each other and in B, cars 3 and 4 will move away.
c In A, cars 1 and 2 will move away and in B, 3 and 4 will come closer to each other.
d In A, cars 1 and 2 will come closer to each other and in B, 3 and 4 will move away from each other.

3. Vicky is trying to magnetize an iron nail using a method as shown in the figure below.

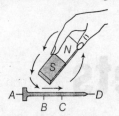

If he succeeds then which part of the iron nail would be the north pole?

a *A*   b *B*
c *C*   d *D*

4. To check whether a piece of metal is a magnet or not, which of the following observation would offer conclusive evidence?

a It attracts a known magnet
b It repels a known magnet
c It attracts a steel screw driver
d None of the above

5. Which of the following diagrams shown below correctly shows the properties of magnets?

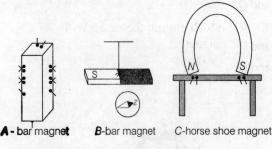

A - bar magnet   *B*-bar magnet   *C*-horse shoe magnet

a *A* and *B*
b *A* and *C*
c *B* and *C*
d *A*, *B* and *C*

6. Three magnets A, B and C were dipped one by one in a heap of iron filing. The figure below shows the amount of the iron filing sticking to them.

The strength of these magnets will be

a *A* > *B* > *C*
b *A* < *B* < *C*
c *A* = *B* = *C*
d *A* < *B* > *C*

7. Fill in the blanks using the suitable option given below.

I. .... is the surest test of magnetism.
II. Similar poles .... each other whereas opposite poles .... each other.
III. .... of a magnet have greatest magnetism.
IV. The .... behaves as a giant magnet buried under at its centre.

Codes

	I	II	III	IV
a	Poles	attract, repel	earth	repulsion
b	Repulsion	repel, attract	poles	earth
c	Repulsion	attract, repel	poles	earth
d	Poles	repel, attract	repulsion	earth

8. State true or false using codes given below.

I. Magnetic lines emerge from south pole and merge at north pole.
II. Bar magnets are stored in pairs with similar poles on same side.
III. Dropping a magnet on floor can affect its magnetism.
IV. Horse shoe magnet contains only one pole.

Codes

	I	II	III	IV
a	F	F	T	F
b	F	T	T	F
c	F	F	F	T
d	F	T	F	T

9. Matrix matching.

A.	N–N	1.	storage of magnets
B.	N–S	2.	demagnetization
C.	Hammering	3.	repulsion
D.	Keepers	4.	attraction

Codes

	A	B	C	D
a	3	4	1	2
b	3	4	2	1
c	4	3	1	2
d	4	3	2	1

10. Assertion (A) The poles of a magnet can never be dissociated.

Reason (R) If you break a bar magnet then each piece will have its own north-south pole.

Select the correct answer from the codes given below.

a Both A and R are correct and R is the correct explanation of A

b Both A and R are correct and R is not the correct explanation of A

c A is true, but R is false

d R is true, but A is false

11. Assertion (A) A freely suspended magnet aligns itself automatically in geographical north-south directions.

Reason (R) Earth behaves as a huge bar magnet buried at its centre.

Select the correct answer from the options given below.

a Both A and R are correct and R is the correct explanation of A

b Both A and R are correct and R is not the correct explanation of A

c A is true, but R is false

d R is true, but A is false

12. Consider the following statements and choose the correct option.

I. Hammering a magnet enhances its magnetism.

II. Heating a magnet enhances its magnetism.

III. A magnet being dropped from a **height** enhances its magnetism.

Codes

a All are correct

b All are incorrect

c Only II is correct

d Both I and III are correct

 Direction (Q.Nos. 13 and 14)

Read the following information and answer the questions that follow

During an experiment a student was provided four identical iron bars. He dipped each bar in a heap of iron filings one by one as shown in the figure below.

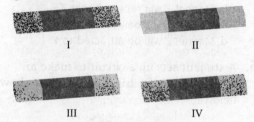

13. Which among the four iron bars are magnets?

a Only I

b II and III

c I and II

d I, III and IV

14. Which among the four bars is the strongest magnet?

a Only I

b Only II

c Only III

d Only IV

B Magnetic Materials and Applications

1. A scrap dealer uses a huge magnet to separate some metals.

Which pair of metals will it be able to pick up?

a Brass and copper

b Aluminium and brass

c Iron and steel

d Cobalt and iron

2. Rohan kept a bar magnet nearby an iron bar. He observed that the iron bar attracts a pin as shown in the figure below.

What could be the reason for the above observation?

a Iron bar becomes magnetic and attracts the pin

b The pin is made up of magnetic material

c Both (a) and (b)

d Neither (a) nor (b)

3. Paheli and her friends were decorating the class bulletin board. She dropped the box of stainless steel pins by mistake. She tried to collect the pins using a magnet. She could not succeed. What could be the reason for this?

a Steel is a magnetic material

b Steel is magnetic only when electric current is passed through it

c Both (a) and (b)

d Neither (a) nor (b)

4. Observe the diagram shown below which consists of two horse shoe magnets and one bar magnet.

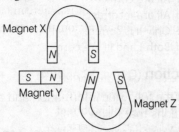

Which statement is true about the following arrangement?

a Magnet X will repel magnet Z
b Magnet Y will repel magnet Z
c Magnet X will be attracted to Y
d Magnet Z will be attracted to Y

5. A student sets up a circuit to make an electromagnet for his experiment as shown below.

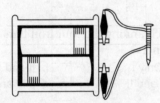

What kind of nail should not be used if he wants to make an electromagnet?

a Iron   b Steel
c Cobalt   d Copper

6. Consider the following statements about magnetism. Which of them is the correct statement?

a A magnet attracts small pieces of aluminium.
b Steel makes a better permanent magnet than iron does.
c There is no limit to the magnetic strength of a magnet made from a steel bar.
d Two like poles always attract one another.

7. Shashank suspended four bars of different materials from a pole. He then brought the north pole of a bar magnet near part X and Y of each bar one by one.

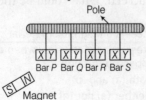

The observations he recorded are as follows

Bar	Magnet and Part X	Magnet and Part Y
P	Pushed	Pulled
Q	Nothing happened	Nothing happened
R	Pulled	Pushed
S	Pulled	Pulled

Which of the following sets correctly represents metal bars P, Q, R and S?

	Bar P	Bar Q	Bar R	Bar S
a	Magnet	Glass bar	Magnet	Iron bar
b	Magnet	Iron bar	Magnet	Copper bar
c	Copper bar	Magnet	Iron bar	Magnet
d	Magnet	Iron bar	Copper bar	Glass bar

8. Fill in the blanks using the suitable codes given below

I. Magnets made by using electric current are known as ....
II. .... is used to make permanent magnets.
III. In order to convert an iron piece into a magnet, we should stroke it with the same .... of a bar magnet in the .... direction repeatedly.
IV. .... is a natural magnet.

Codes

	I	II	III	IV
a	Loadstone	steel	pole, same	electro-magnets
b	electromagnets	loadstone	same, pole	steel
c	loadstone	electro-magnets	pole, same	steel
d	electromagnets	steel	pole, same	loadstone

9. State true or false using codes given below.

I. Alloy like alnico is used in making temporary magnet.
II. Magnet is used in CD's and DVD's.
III. Electromagnets are used for removing brass pieces from a scrap of brass and copper.
IV. A mixture of iron and aluminium powder can be separated using a magnet.

Codes

	I	II	III	IV
a	T	F	T	T
b	F	T	F	T
c	F	F	F	T
d	T	F	F	F

10. Matrix matching.

	Column I		Column II
A.	Magnetic materials	1.	loadstone
B.	Magnetic needle	2.	air and water
C.	Natural magnets	3.	cobalt and nickel
D.	Non-magnetic materials	4.	soft iron

Codes

	A	B	C	D
a	1	2	3	4
b	2	3	4	1
c	3	4	1	2
d	4	3	2	1

11. Assertion (A) Electromagnets are used in door bells.

Reason (R) Electromagnets are functional only when current is passed through the magnetic material.

Select the correct answer from the options given below.

a Both (A) and (R) are correct and (R) is the correct explanation of (A)

b Both (A) and (R) are correct and (R) is not the correct explanation of (A)

c (A) is true, but (R) is false

d (R) is true, but (A) is false

12. Assertion (A) Magnets are used to separate iron and steel from nickel.

Reason (R) Materials which are attracted by a magnet are known as magnetic materials example iron.

Select the correct answer from the options given below.

a Both (A) and (R) are correct and (R) is the correct explanation of (A)

b Both (A) and (R) are correct and (R) is not the correct explanation of (A)

c (A) is true, but (R) is false

d (R) is true, but (A) is false

13. Consider the following statements and choose the correct option.

   I. Attraction is a sure test for magnetism.

   II. Repulsion is a sure test for magnetism.

   III. Both repulsion and attraction are sure test for magnetism.

Codes

a I and II are correct III is incorrect

b I and III are correct II is incorrect

c I and II are incorrect III is correct

d I and III are incorrect II is correct

14. Solve the following crossword using hints given below.

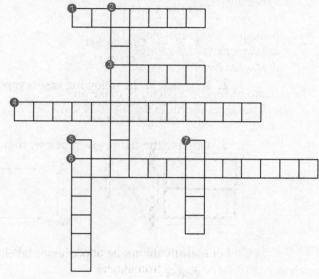

Across

   1. It is an instrument which uses a magnet to detect directions

   3. Magnetic lines of force originate from this pole

   4. The region in which magnetic force can be experienced

   6. Magnets made by using electricity

Downard

   2. Magnets are obtained from these rocks

   5. These are used to store the bar magnets

   7. The ends of a magnet are known as

Water

Chapter **12**

1. The quantity of water required to produce __A__ page of your book is __B__. Identify A and B.

	A	B			A	B
a	2	— One bucket	b	4	— Ten buckets
c	1	— 2 glasses	d	3	— 1 glass

2. In which of the following case, evaporation of water will be slowest?
   - a A tray of water kept in sunlight
   - b A kettle of water kept on a burner
   - c A glass of water kept in room
   - d A bucket of water kept on roof top

3. Observe the figure given below, that shows changes in state that water goes through.

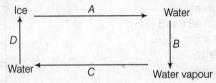

   Identify the name of processes labelled as A, B, C and D.

   Codes

	A	B	C	D
a	Evaporation	Melting	Condensation	Freezing
b	Melting	Condensation	Evaporation	Freezing
c	Melting	Evaporation	Condensation	Freezing
d	Condensation	Evaporation	Melting	Freezing

4. The diagram below shows two bottles that have water droplets formed on them.

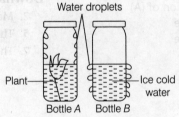

   Which of the following is responsible for the formation of droplets on bottle B?
   - a Water vapour from the surroundings touches the cooled surface of bottle B and condenses to form tiny water droplets
   - b Water droplets form due to the process of transpiration
   - c Water droplets form due to temperature variation
   - d Water vapour from the surroundings touches the surface of bottle B and evaporation to form water droplets

5. Priyanka hanged her clothes after washing to dry.

denim jeans   cotton T-shirt   beach towel   cotton scarf

Observe the figures to identify the cloth that take longest time for drying and reason behind this delay.

	Clothes	Reason
a	Cotton T-shirt	Rate of condensation
b	Cotton scarf	Rate of evaporation
c	Denim jeans	Rate of evaporation
d	Beach towel	Rate of condensation

6. Study the diagram of the water cycle below:

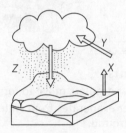

Which of the following correctly represent X, Y and Z ?

	X	Y	Z
a	Condensation	Evaporation	Snow/Rain
b	Condensation	Snow	Evaporation
c	Snow	Evaporation	Condensation
d	Evaporation	Condensation	Snow/Rain

7. Fishes are kept in aquarium A and B. Aquarium A contains tap water while B contains boiled water. The fishes in aquarium B died while those in aquarium A were alive. Which of the following is the correct reason behind this?

Aquarium A

Aquarium B

a Aquarium A contains pure water
b There were too many impurities in aquarium B
c Water in aquarium A contains more dissolved oxygen
d Water in aquarium B contains dissolved gases

8. There are some water resources given below. They are arranged in an incorrect manner, on the basis of their drinkability from most drinkable to undrinkable water. Opt the option that declares the correct order.

Sequence

Rain	Lake	Spring	Sea
I	II	III	IV

a I → III → II → IV
b IV → II → III → I
c I → II → III → IV
d II → III → I → IV

9. Read the given statements about water.
1. Sound travels faster through water than air.
2. Pure water is salty.
3. Ice sinks in water.
4. Water is not easy to compress.
5. Water is an example of chemical element.

Which of these are correct.

a 1 and 2
b 1 and 4
c 2, 3 and 5
d 3, 4 and 1

10. Observe the given flow chart and opt the correct statement regarding it.

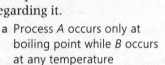
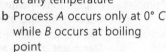
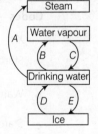

a Process A occurs only at boiling point while B occurs at any temperature
b Process A occurs only at 0° C while B occurs at boiling point
c Process A occurs at any temperature while B occurs at 0°C only
d Both process occur at 0°C only

11. Nidhi set-up an experiment to obtain pure water from seawater. Study the experimental set-up and answer the question that follows.

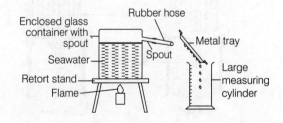

What will happen if the metal tray is replaced by a tray made of wood?

    a Result will be same with both metal tray and wooden tray

    b Steam would not condense into water droplets on the wooden surface

    c Steam would condense more into water droplets on the wooden surface

    d Steam would not condense into water droplet's metal tray

12. Vandana removed the peel of an apple and sliced it into chunks. She kept the chunks of apple in a transparent beaker and placed a layer of plastic cling over the opening. The beaker was then heated over flame.

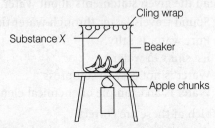

After a while, substance X could be seen on the inside surface of the cling wrap.

    (i) Identify substance X.

    (ii) How did substance X form?

Codes

	X	Substance X formation
a	Starch droplet	Apple chunks heated → Starch get evaporated
b	Water droplet	Apple chunks heated → Water get evaporated
c	Starch droplet	Apple chunks heated → Starch get condensed
d	Water droplet	Apple chunks heated → Water get condensed

13. Robby conducted an experiment with two liquids as shown in the setup below:

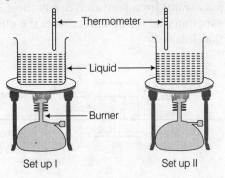

The two set ups were continuously given heat from the burner. Which of the set up contains water as liquid?

    a In set up II, the thermometer reading keeps on rising. This shows it contains water

    b The reading of the thermometer stops rising after 100° C in set up I. This shows it has water

    c Both the setups contain water as the thermometer reading stopped at 90° C

    d None of the setups has water, there was no rise in temperature reading with time

14. Study the water cycle and given statements carefully.

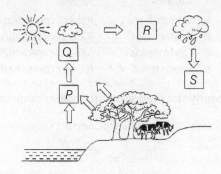

Statements

    A. Water droplets move to form bigger clouds.

    B. Water evaporates from water bodies and the ground.

    C. Rain fall onto the land and is collected in water bodies.

    D. Water vapour rises into the sky, cools and condenses to form clouds.

Relate P, Q, R and S of the cycles with statements A, B, C and D correctly.

Codes

	P	Q	R	S		P	Q	R	S
a	A	B	C	D	b	D	C	B	A
c	C	D	B	A	d	B	D	A	C

15. Three identical handkerchiefs, A, B and C, were soaked in water and were hanged on a washing line as shown below for half an hour.

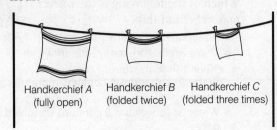

Handkerchief A (fully open)   Handkerchief B (folded twice)   Handkerchief C (folded three times)

Identify the factors that could affect the rate of evaporation of water from the handkerchiefs.

Codes
a Air, water
b Temperature, wind, water
c Climate, air
d Temperature, wind, humidity

16. Observe and study the given flow chart and identify A, B and C

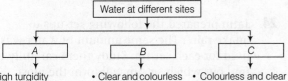

| | Water at different sites | |
| A | B | C |

- High turgidity
- Low total dissolved solids (TDS)
- Low alkalinity
- Low hardness
- Low chloride fluoride content
- High Level of bacteria

- Clear and colourless
- High total dissolved solids (TDS)
- High alkalinity
- High hardness
- High chloride fluoride content
- Low level of bacteria

- Colourless and clear
- High total dissolved solids (TDS)
- Low alkalinity
- Low hardness
- Low chloride, fluoride content
- Low level of bacteria

Codes

	A	B	C
a	Surface water	Subsoil water in river beds	Ground water
b	Ground water	Sea water	Subsoil water in river beds
c	Surface water	Ground water	Subsoil water in river beds
d	Sea water	Surface water	Ground water

17.

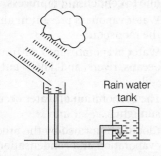

Rain water tank

The above figure is a line diagram of rain harvesting system. Observe the figure and identify the correct option regarding it.

I. The concentration of contaminants is reduced significantly by diverting the initial flow of runoff water to ground.

II. The water collected is just redirected to deep percolation pit where it is filtered.

III. The harvested water can never be used for drinking but used for irrigation.

IV. Rainwater harvesting provides an independent water supply for potable water.

Codes
a I and II
b I, II and III
c III and IV
d I, II and IV

18. Vicky packed some hot fried noodles into a container for his lunch break. Before he left for school, he observed that water droplets had formed in the container. Which of the diagrams below shows the formation of water droplets in the container correctly?

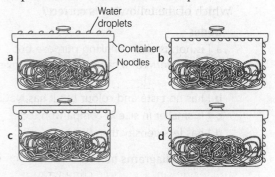

19. Four identical towels were hanged out to dry under different conditions.

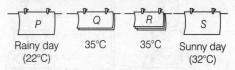

Rainy day (22°C)   35°C   35°C   Sunny day (32°C)

Arrange them in order, beginning with the towel that would take the longest time to dry.

a P, Q, R, S
b P, R, Q, S
c R, P, Q, S
d S, Q, R, P

20. Swati wants to find out if the temperature of water will affect the amount of salt that will dissolve in the water. She sets up the experiment as shown below.

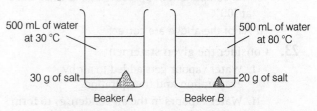

500 mL of water at 30 °C
500 mL of water at 80 °C
30 g of salt
20 g of salt
Beaker A
Beaker B

The experiment is not a fair test. What must she do to the set-ups to make it a fair test?

A. Add 10 g of salt to beaker *B*.
B. Add 50 mL of water into beaker *A*.
C. Remove 50 mL of water from beaker *B*.
D. Increase the temperature of water in beaker *A* to 80°C.

Codes
a Only *A*
b *A* and *B*
c *B*, *C* and *D*
d *A*, *B*, *C* and *D*

21. Consider the given labellings:
    I. Sea water.
    II. River and lake water.

    Which of the following is correct?

    Codes
    a I is not used for drinking purpose but filtered form of II can be used for drinking easily.
    b I has no taste and colour but II has NaCl in it.
    c I is smaller in size in comparison to II.
    d I has less density than II.

22. Study the diagrams below.

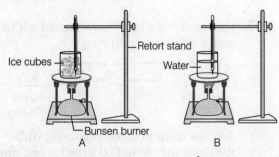

    Which of the following is correct regarding the above?
    a The component of *A* and *B* are losing heat in both set-ups
    b In *A*, ice will change into vapours directly and in *B*, water will change into steam
    c The component of *B* freezes at 0°C while boils at 100°C
    d All of the above are correct

23. Consider the given statements:
    I. Water vapour gets added to air by evaporation and transpiration.
    II. Water vapours in the air condenses to form tiny droplets of water which appears as clouds.

III. Hail helps in replenishment of water.
IV. Excessive rainfall may cause droughts.
 V. Circulation of water between ocean and land is called precipitation.

Which of the following are incorrect from above statements?

Codes
a III and V
b I, III, IV and V
c IV and V
d Only V

24. Jatin prepared the following set-ups to 'make rain'. The same amount of water was used for each set-up. Study them carefully to find out which set-up will form the most 'rain'?

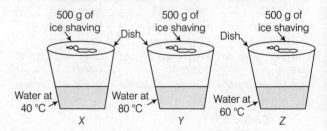

a *X*
b *Y*
c *Z*
d None of the above

25. Consider the given statements and opt the option that correctly declares them either true or false.
    I. Fog appearing on a cold winter morning is due to condensation process.
    II. Water vapour is present in air only during the monsoon.
    III. Water evaporates into air from the oceans, rivers and lakes but not from soil.
    IV. The evaporation of water occurs fastest in sunlight.
    V. Clouds are formed by the process of evaporation and condensation.

Codes

	I	II	III	IV	V
a	F	T	T	T	F
b	T	F	F	T	T
c	F	F	T	T	T
d	T	F	F	F	T

26. Assertion (A) Drinking water is called as potable water.

Reason (R) It is free from contaminants.

Consider the above A and R and choose the correct option.

    a Both A and R are true and R is the correct explanation of A

    b Both A and R are true, but R is not the correct explanation of A

    c A is true, but R is false

    d Both A and R are true

27. Solve the following crossword with the help of given clues.

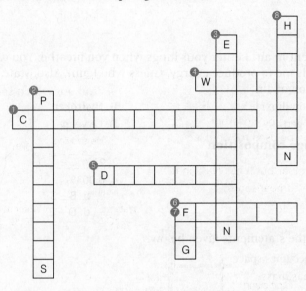

Across

    1. Process of changing water vapour into water.

    4. It is a universal solvent.

    5. No rainfall for more than a year leads to .... in the region.

    7. Excessive rainfall leads to.

Down

    2. The contaminants that pollute air, water, soil, etc.

    3. Process to changing water into its vapour state.

    6. Whitish air that appears in winters.

    8. Apart from oxygen, water has two molecules of.

Chapter 13

Air

1. I am present in air. I enter your lungs when you breathe. You cannot live without me. Your body needs me to produce energy. Guess who I am? Also, state the percentage I have in composition of air.

    A. Carbon dioxide   B. Hydrogen

    C. Nitrogen   D. Oxygen

Percentage composition

    1. 78%   2. 21%

    3. 1%   4. 0.003%

    a A – 4   b B – 3

    c C – 1   d D – 2

2. Consider the statements given below.

    I. Air occupies space.

    II. Air has mass.

    III. Air dissolves in water to support the life of aquatic animals.

    IV. Air does not have colour, odour or taste.

    V. Air is compressible.

Which of the above statement(s) is/are incorrect ?

    a Only II   b II and V

    c Only V   d None of these

3. Select the option which on reshuffling will give the name of atmospheric layer that contain the ozone layer for absorption of UV rays.

    a rephosrtsate   b ereroostph

    c oozoeerpnh   d phlieerpthso

4. The air pollution on the road can be reduced by which of the following?

    I. Use of bicycles in place of fuel cars.

    II. Planting trees on roadsides.

    III. Using CNG based vehicles.

    IV. Walking more than driving.

    V. Using unleaded petrol in cars.

Codes

    a I, II, III and IV   b I, II, IV and V

    c I, III, IV and V   d I, II, III, IV and V

5. Air is made up of a mixture of gases which is shown in the form of a pie chart. Identify A, B and C.

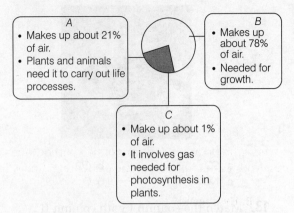

A
- Makes up about 21% of air.
- Plants and animals need it to carry out life processes.

B
- Makes up about 78% of air.
- Needed for growth.

C
- Make up about 1% of air.
- It involves gas needed for photosynthesis in plants.

Codes

	A	B	C
a	Nitrogen	Oxygen	Carbon dioxide, rare gases and water vapour
b	Oxygen	Nitrogen	Carbon dioxide, rare gases and water vapour
c	Oxygen	Carbon dioxide	Nitrogen, rare gases and water vapour
d	Nitrogen	Oxygen	Carbon monoxide, rare gases and water vapour

6. Consider the given statements and answer the following questions.

I. When fewer plants are available to take in carbon dioxide from the air, the amount of carbon dioxide increases.

II. Carbon dioxide retains heat near the earth's surface and increases the temperature of earth.

On the basis of the above information. Identify the best suitable option for defining the nature of carbon dioxide.

a CO_2 is an air pollutant
b CO_2 is a greenhouse gas
c CO_2 is not a part of healthy air
d All of the above

7. Observe the flow chart given below carefully and identify P, Q and S.

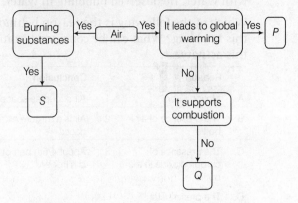

Codes

	P	Q	S
a	CO_2	N_2	O_2
b	O_2	CO_2	N_2
c	CO	O_2	N_2
d	O_2	N_2	CO_2

8. Observe the figure given below, carefully and identify A, B and C.

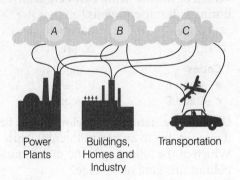

Power Plants   Buildings, Homes and Industry   Transportation

Codes

	A	B	C
a	O_2	N_2	SO_2
b	CO_2	CO	N_2
c	SO_2	CO_2	NO_x
d	N_2	SO_x	CO

9. Ujjawal takes an empty glass bottle. He dip the open mouth of the bottle into the bucket filled with water. He observed bubbling in water.

Which of the following is the reason behind this bubbling? What can be concluded from this activity?

	Reason		Conclusion
A.	Motion in air	1.	Air occupies space
B.	The presence of air in bottle	2.	Air is a mixture of gases
C.	The presence of carbon dioxide in the bottle	3.	About 4/5th part of air is nitrogen
D.	The presence of oxygen in the bottle		

Choose the correct combination.

  a A – 2   **b** B – 1
  c C – 1   **d** D – 3

10. While watching news, Shibu saw a news of volcanic eruption in country XYZ.

Next day, he asked his teacher, "Is there any gas that is emitted during volcanic eruption ?" His teacher replied – Yes.

Which of the following gases are emitted in during volcanic eruptions?

  A. Ozone   B. NO_x
  C. CO_2 D. SO_x

  Codes
  a A and B   **b** B and C
  c C and D   **d** A and C

11. Observe the statue given below. It has been damaged due to an environmental cause. Which of the following is the major cause behind this kind of damage?

  Codes
  a Ozone depletion
  b Global warming
  c Acid rain
  d Air pollution

12. The gas stove as shown in the figure below, on ignition produces a gas which acts as an air pollutant ? Which gas is this?

  a SO_x **b** CO
  c NO_x **d** O_3

13. Match the column I with column II.

	Column I		Column II
A.	Troposphere	1.	30 miles above the surface of earth
B.	Stratosphere	2.	Coldest layer
C.	Mesosphere	3.	300 miles above the earth
D.	Thermosphere	4.	Satellites circles the earth here, fades into space
E.	Exosphere	5.	10 miles above the surface of the earth

  Codes

	A	B	C	D	E			A	B	C	D	E
a	1	2	3	4	5		**b**	5	1	2	3	4
c	5	2	3	1	4		**d**	1	5	4	3	2

14. Which of the following statements is/are correct ?

  A. Acid rain that causes damage to buildings, is formed due to air pollution.

  B. Plants and animals depend on each other for exchange of oxygen and carbon dioxide from air.

  C. Ozone layer protects us from UV radiations coming from sun.

  D. Pure water is a translucent liquid.

  Codes
  a A and B
  b B and C
  c C and D
  d Both a and b

15.

I	II	III	IV
Sulphur oxides	N_2	CFCs	Smoke
V	VI	VII	VIII
Nitrogen oxides	CO	O_2	Coal
IX	X	XI	XII
Water vapour	Lead	Mercury	Smog

Which of the above compounds do not act as air pollutants?

a VII, VIII, IX
b VI, VII, IX, XI
c II, VII, IX
d II, VII, IX, XII

16. Consider the statement given below:

Record snowfall disproves global warming.

Which of the following justifies the above statement?

a CO_2 is increasing rapidly.
b Warming leads to increased evaporation and precipitation.
c Ozone is depleting.
d None of the above

17. We usually observe that air becomes clean after rainfall (as shown in the figure below). Which of the following is the correct reason behind it?

Before rainfall   After rainfall

a Rain catches all the pollution on its way down.
b Sun shines more after rain.
c Due to acid rain.
d Due to global warming.

18.

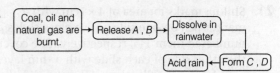

Above chain of events shows the formation of acid. Identify A, B, C and D components to complete the chain.

Codes

	A	B	C	D
a	Sulphur dioxide	Nitrogen	Sulphuric acid	Nitric acid
b	Sulphur	Nitrogen oxide	Sulphuric acid	Ammonia
c	Carbon monoxide	Sulphur dioxide	Sulphuric acid	CFCs
d	Sulphur dioxide	Nitrogen oxide	Sulphuric acid	Nitric acid

19. Match the column I with column II.

	Column I		Column II
A.	Nitrogen	1.	Glass with ice cold H_2O
B.	Oxygen	2.	Needed by plants to grow
C.	Carbon dioxide	3.	Harmful for living organisms
D.	Dust and smoke	4.	Needed for respiration
E.	Water vapour	5.	Constitute about 0.03% in air composition

Codes

	A	B	C	D	E			A	B	C	D	E
a	1	3	4	2	5		b	2	4	5	3	1
c	2	4	1	3	5		d	1	4	3	2	5

20. Consider the given statements and opt the option that correctly declares them either true or false.

I. Air cannot be seen or felt.
II. Air occupies space and has mass.
III. Combustion occurs only in the presence of nitrogen.
IV. Deep sea divers carry oxygen cylinders along with them when they go deep into the sea.
V. Plants need oxygen for respiration.

Codes

	I	II	III	IV	V
a	T	T	T	F	T
b	T	T	F	T	F
c	T	T	F	F	T
d	T	T	T	F	T

21. Shikha marks an area of 4 × 1 cm with a marker pen on one side of five glass slides and numbered them 1-5, respectively. She covers the other side of each slide with a thin layer of petroleum jelly. She then taped the slide to five different sites (petroleum jelly facing outward) as shown in the figure.

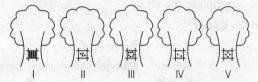

Which of the following slide was kept in most polluted site ?

a I and V b Only I c Only III d Only II

22. The figure given below shows the smoke emitted by coal and oil burnt in factories and power stations below it, a list of some compounds is given.

A. Ozone   B. Sulphur dioxide
C. Sodium bicarbonate   D. CFCs
E. PAN   F. Nitrogen dioxide

Which of the above air pollutants are most commonly released by industries?

a B, C, D and E   b B and F
c D and E   d All of these

23. Read the steps of an experiment below.
I. Fill one-third of a tub with water (mixed with caustic soda and ink).
II. Place a burning candle in it.
III. Cover the tub with a jar which does not allow the air to pass in the tub.
IV. After sometime, the candle will stop burning and coloured water will rise to fill the vacuum form by the burning of air components.

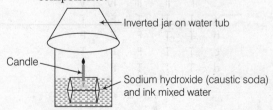

Which of the following is the component of air that burns and the reason behind–why water rises to fill the vacuum?

	Component	Reason
a	Carbon dioxide	absorption of carbon dioxide by caustic soda
b	Oxygen	absorption of oxygen by caustic soda
c	Carbon dioxide	absorption of oxygen by caustic soda
d	Oxygen	absorption of carbon dioxide by caustic soda

24. Which of the following is incorrect ?

	Layer of earth's atmosphere	Location (↑–above the earth)	Information / Description
A.	Troposphere	10 km↑	Weather balloons fly in this layer.
B.	Stratosphere	80 km↑	Supersonic planes fly in this layer.
C.	Mesosphere	50 km↑	Ionosphere is located in this layer.
D.	Thermosphere	240 km↑	It has temperature about 2400°C during day.
E.	Exosphere	Outer layer of earth	Rate of atmospheric particles collision is less

(↑ above the earth)

Codes

a A, B and C   b B and D
c Only D   d Only B

25. Read the following statements and mark the option that correctly states them as true (T) or false (F).
I. The proportion of CO_2 in cities is greater in air than in rural areas.
II. The air becomes thicker with attitude.
III. Windmill uses the power of air to generate electricity.
IV. Dust is essential for cloud formation.
V. The lower the temperature, lower is the solubility of air in water.

Codes

	I	II	III	IV	V
a	T	T	T	F	T
b	F	T	F	F	F
c	T	T	T	F	F
d	T	F	F	T	F

26. There is a condition given below. Opt the correct reason in support of the condition from the options that follow.

Condition

There is an incident of fire and a person is caught by that fire. Other person came to help and wrapped him in woollen blanket.

    Codes
    a To cut off the supply of carbon dioxide from air. b To cut off the supply of oxygen present in air.
    c To cut off the supply of nitrogen present in air.   d None of the above

27. Joan conducted an experiment from 10 am to 3 pm. An *Elodea* plant was placed in jar X and a water snail was placed in a similar jar Y. Both jars were placed in the garden where there was sunlight.

Jar X   Jar Y

Which of the following correctly shows the changes in the amount of dissolved oxygen in each jar over time?

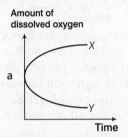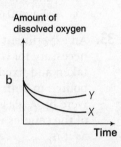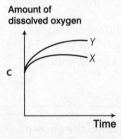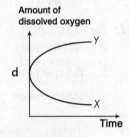

28. Roshni conducted an experiment to find out which type of habitat is most suitable for earthworms. Her experimental set-ups are as

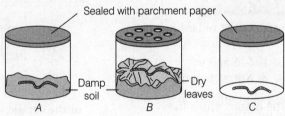

After two weeks in which of the containers will she find the earthworm still alive ?
  a Only A   b Only B   c A and C   d A, B and C

29. Observe the tabulated form of information given below about air pollution. Identify *P, Q, R, S* and *T*.

	Major sources	Health effects	Environmental effects
P	Industry	Respiratory and cardiovascular illness	Precursor to acid rain which damages lakes, rivers and trees; damage to cultural relics
Q	Vehicles; Industry	Respiratory and cardiovascular illness	Nitrogen deposition leading to over-fertilisation and eutrophication
PM	Vehicles; Industry	Particles penetrate deep into lungs and can enter bloodstream	Visibility
R	Vehicles	Headaches and fatigue, especially in people with weak cardiovascular health	Poisonous in nature
S	Formed from reaction of NO_X and VOCs	Respiratory illness	Reduced crop production and forest growth; smog precursor
T	Vehicles; Industrial processes	Eye and skin irritation; nausea; headaches; carcinogenic	Smog precursor

	P	Q	R	S	T
a	NO$_X$	SO$_2$	CO	VOCs	Ozone
b	SO$_2$	NO$_X$	CO	Ozone	VOCs
c	CO	SO$_2$	NO$_X$	Ozone	VOCs
d	NO$_X$	CO	SO$_2$	VOCs	Ozone

30. Observe the tabulated form of information given below which involves some chemical compounds and related atmospheric problems.

	Atmospheric problems	SO$_2$	NO$_X$	NH$_3$	VOC	CO	CH$_4$
A.	Photochemical smog	+	+	−	+	+	+
B.	Winter smog	+	+	−	−	−	−
C.	Acidification	+	+	+	−	+	−
D.	Eutrophication	−	+	+	−	−	−
E.	Climate change	−	+	−	+	+	+

Key (+ : involved in causing the respective atmospheric problem)

(− : not involved in causing the respective atmospheric problem)

Which of the following is correct regarding the given table?

a A, B and D
b C, D and E
c B, C and D
d A, B, C, D and E

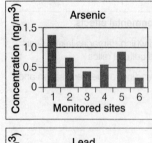 **Direction** (Q. No. 31) The graphs show the concentrations of different pollutants detected in air samples at six monitored sites in suburban areas.

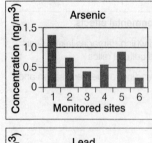
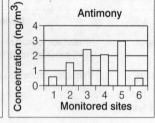
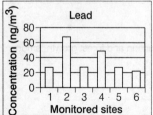
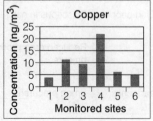

31. The smelting of copper ore releases copper and lead pollutants into the air.
Which two sites are most likely to be near copper ore smelters?

a Sites 3 and 6
b Sites 2 and 3
c Sites 2 and 4
d Sites 4 and 6

32. Which of the following steps can reduce the problem of pollution?

A. Recycling paper, aluminium tins and glasswares.
B. Using unleaded petrol.
C. Producing charcoal as a fuel source.
D. Destroying pests by using pesticides.

a A and B
b B and D
c A, B and D
d A, C and D

33. An experiment was conducted to check if air is necessary for combustion. Two candles were taken and fixed in a plastic trough. Water was poured in both the troughs and the candles were lit. A glass tumbler was inverted over one of the candles while the other candle was left as it is.

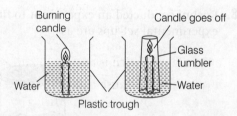

It was observed that after sometime the flame of the candle with glass tumbler inverted over it started to flicker and finally went off. The other candle continued to burn until the candle reaches the level of water. What do you conclude from this experiment?

a Air is essential for combustion.
b Air is not essential for combustion.
c Nitrogen which is a component of air is essential for combustion.
d None of the above

34. Assertion (A) New cars are less polluting than older ones.

Reason (R) They are fitted with a device that changes the exhaust gases into nitrogen.

a Both A and R are true and R is the correct explanation of A
b Both A and R are true, but R is not the correct explanation of A
c A is true, but R is false
d Both A and R are false

35. In the set up given below, one of the balloons was picked. It was observed that the side of the metre scale with the air filled balloon went down.

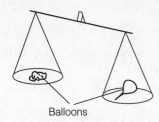

Balloons

What can be inferred from this experiment ?

a Air has no weight.
b Air has weight of its own.
c Air has the same weight as that of the object in which it is filled.
d None of the above

36. Consider the given passage and opt the option that correctly fill its gaps.

The envelope of air around the earth is called ____(i)____. Earth has different layers of atmosphere. ____(ii)____ covers the large part of the earth atmosphere, which is about 120 km above the mesopause and below the ____(iii)____. The atmospheric particles in this layer become electrically charged which support the ____(iv)____ waves for the reception in the space. In this region a zone is called an acoustic zone prevents the transmission of ____(v)____.

Codes

	(i)	(ii)	(iii)	(iv)	(v)
a	Atmosphere	Thermosphere	Exosphere	Radio	Sound
b	Oxygen	Atmosphere	Troposphere	Ultra violet	Electr-ons
c	Stratosphere	Thermosphere	Mesosphere	Radio	Sound
d	Ozonosphere	Stratosphere	Thermosphere	Ultra violet	Electro ns

37. Solve the puzzle with the help of given clues.

Across

1. Gas needed by plants for photosynthesis.
5. Mountaineers carry it in cylinder.
6. Aquatic animals use dissolved air in water for —.
8. Element present 78% in air.

Down

2. Air in motion is called —.
3. Envelope of air that surrounds the earth.
4. It is a mixture of several gases.
7. It is shown by weather cock, when air moves.

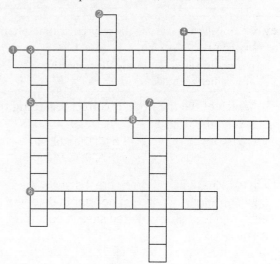

Practice
Sets

Practice Set ①

A Whole Content Based Test for Class 6th Science Olympiad

1. Look at the diagram below.

Which one of the following shows the correct reflection of the picture card on the mirror?

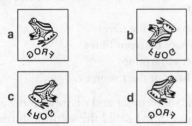

a   b

c   d

2. Rahul and Shubham went for a school trip with their friends and school teachers. They reached at a place, where it was very cold.

They saw many kinds of trees which are of cone-shaped and their leaves were of needle-shaped, that were very different from the ones near their home. At which region they were for their trip?
   a Mountain region of Himalaya
   b Sea beach region of Gujarat
   c Plain region of Thar
   d None of the above

3. The diagram shows a magnet that is being used to pick up a steel bar. The N-pole of the magnet is close to the centre Y of the steel bar as shown. What are the poles induced in the steel bar at X, Y and Z?

	Pole induced (at X)	Pole induced (at Y)	Pole induced (at Z)
a	N	N	N
b	N	S	N
c	S	N	S
d	S	S	S

4. James was given a cube-like sponge and a cylindrical container. He was able to squeeze the whole sponge into the cylindrical container.

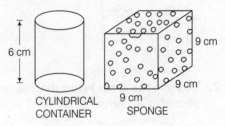

6 cm

9 cm

9 cm

9 cm

CYLINDRICAL CONTAINER   SPONGE

From the above experiment, he concluded that the sponge is
   a a liquid as its shape changes
   b a solid as have definite dimensions
   c a gas, as the shape and size both change
   d a liquid, as the shape and size both change

5. Which of the following is incorrect?
   I. Vitamin-D is synthesised by skin in our body.
   II. Iodine is essential for the working of our thyroid gland.
   III. Eating spinach is good for us, as it provides phosphorus in rich quantity.
   IV. In take of folic acid causes anaemia.
   V. Fats give more energy than that of carbohydrates.

   Codes
   a III and IV
   b III, IV and V
   c I, III and IV
   d I and IV

6. Which of the following shows the correct way of connecting an ammeter and a voltmeter?

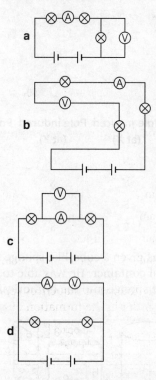

7. Observe the given below diagram and identify the correct name for X.

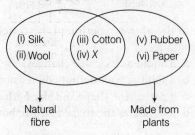

Codes
a Polyester   b Coir
c Cashmere   d Nylon

8. The pictures below show two different pairs of shoes.

Wooden track   Canvas track
shoes   shoes

Marie decides to wear the canvas track shoes rather than the wooden track shoes for the marathon. Which statement(s) would explain her choice of shoes?

I. They are softer and therefore easier to jog with.

II. They are transparent so that she can see, if her feet are suited for the shoes.

III. They are waterproof.

IV. They are handy and will last for a longer period of time.

Codes
a Only I   b II and III
c I and III   d I, II and IV

9. Consider the two groups of fibres
Group 1 : Cotton, Jute, Flax
Group 2 : Fur, Leather, Silk

Which of the following can act as a basis of this grouping?
a Air space inside fibres
b Air space between fibres
c Water absorption
d The basis of their sources

10. Rama took some sugar and dissolve some amount of it in water. She heated the solution formed in experiment I by taking it in a China dish. Then, she heated the sugar alone by taking it in a China dish in experiment II.

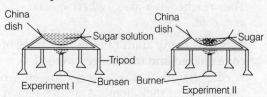

The correct statement about the changes occurring in the above two experiments is
a Experiment I involves a physical change whereas, experiment II involves a chemical change
b Experiment I involves a chemical change whereas experiment II involves a physical change
c Both the experiments involve a physical change
d Both the experiments involve a chemical change

Practice Set 1

11. A food pyramid represents the relative amount of energy in the trophic levels. Which of the following correctly shows a food pyramid?

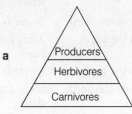

a

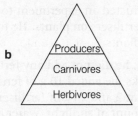

b

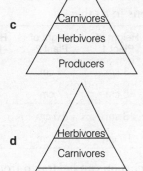

c

d

12. Match the column I with column II.

	Column I		Column II
A.	Wheat	1.	Sugarcane
B.	Sugar	2.	Cow, buffalo and goat
C.	Kheer	3.	Sheep, goat and chicken
D.	Milk	4.	Milk, rice and sugar
E.	Meat	5.	Edible part is seed
		6.	Rice grains and water

Codes

	A	B	C	D	E
a	6	2	3	5	4
b	6	4	1	2	3
c	5	1	2	4	3
d	5	1	4	2	3

13. In the diagram shown below, Mohit studied the shadows of the coconut tree at different times in a day.

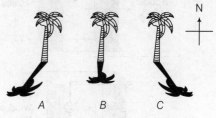

Which of the following options represent the timings correctly?

	A	B	C
a	9 pm	12 pm	4 am
b	10 am	12 am	5 pm
c	10 pm	1 pm	5 am
d	10 am	12 pm	5 pm

14. Which of the following sequences represents the correct order in the formation of a fruit?

a | Fruit → Flower → Dropping of petals → Bud

b | Fruit → Dropping of petals → Flower → Bud

c | Bud → Flower → Dropping of petals → Fruit

d | Bud → Flower → Fruit → Dropping of petals

15. The following arrangements are set-up to store two bar magnets. Which one of them is the correct arrangement?

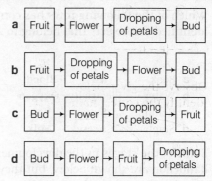

a   Wooden Block / Metal Plates

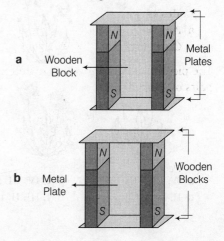

b   Metal Plate / Wooden Blocks

Practice Set 1

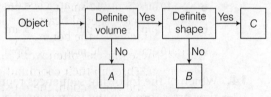

c — Wooden Block, Metal Plates (N S / S N diagram)

d — Metal Plate, Wooden Blocks (N S / S N diagram)

16. Study the flow chart below.

Object → Definite volume → Yes → Definite shape → Yes → C

Definite volume → No → A

Definite shape → No → B

Which of the following rows has correctly identified the objects that belong to *A*, *B* and *C*?

	A	B	C
a	Book	Air	Blood
b	Water	Electricity	Oxygen
c	Helium	Syrup	Vase
d	Stapler	Cheese	Milk

17. Some of the stages in the development of dandelion are shown below, but they are out of order. What is the correct order of the pictures?

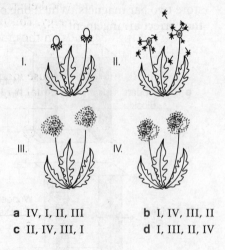

I.   II.   III.   IV.

a IV, I, II, III   **b** I, IV, III, II
c II, IV, III, I   **d** I, III, II, IV

18. If a seed is inserted upside down, into in which direction will its stem and roots grow?

	Stem	Root
a	Away from the Earth	Towards the Earth
b	Towards the Earth	Away from the Earth
c	Towards the Earth	Towards the Earth
d	Away from the Earth	Away from the Earth

19. Nitin conducted an experiment to see the effect of fertilisers on plants. He took three different plants.

To plant 1, he did not add any fertiliser. For 4 weeks, he added 10 g of fertiliser per day to plant 2 and 20 g of fertiliser to plant 3. The amount of sunlight, water and other conditions were kept the same for all the three plants. Nitin recorded his observations in a table.

Weeks	Height of Plant 1	Height of Plant 2	Height of Plant 3
Week 1	3 cm	4 cm	5 cm
Week 2	5 cm	7 cm	8 cm
Week 3	8 cm	10 cm	11 cm
Week 4	10 cm	15 cm	17 cm

What conclusion can be drawn from the observations?

  a Fertilisers reduce the growth of plants.
  b Fertilisers have no effect on the growth of plants.
  c Fertilisers enhance the growth of plants.
  d None of the above

20. The hands and legs are constructed in same pattern as described below.

	Parts of Hand	Parts of Leg	Number of Bones
1.	Upper arm	Thigh	One long bone
2.	Forearm	Lower leg	B
3.	Wrist	Ankle	C
4.	Palm	Foot	D
5.	Fingers	Toe	E

Practice Set 1

Identify B, C, D and E in the given table.

	B	C	D	E
a	1 long bone	2 smaller bones	5 bones	Each has 3 small bones
b	1 long bone	3 smaller bones	5 muscles	3 large bones
c	2 long bones	Several small bones	5 bones	Each has 3 small bones
d	2 long bones	1 small bone	5 ligaments	3 large bones

21. Rohan cut out four sheets of the same size from four different materials; clear plastic, cardboard, frosted glass and metal. He then lined them in a straight line as shown below.

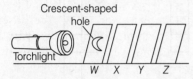

He also cut out a crescent-shaped hole from Sheet W. If he wanted to see a bright crescent-shaped patch of light on Sheet Y only, which one of the following shows the arrangement of the sheets correctly?

	W	X	Y	Z
a	Frosted glass	Metal	Cardboard	Clear plastic
b	Metal	Clear plastic	Frosted glass	Cardboard
c	Cardboard	Frosted glass	Metal	Clear plastic
d	Cardboard	Clear plastic	Metal	Frosted glass

Directions (Q. Nos. 22-25) Study the table given below and answer the questions that follow:

P	Q	R	S
Pen	T-shirt	Notebooks	Fruits
Mug	Vest	Magazines	Vegetables
Toy car	Pants	T	Medicines
Television	Saree	Books	Rubber

22. In the given table, we can replace P by
   a wood   **b** plastic
   c paper   **d** glass

23. In the given table, we can replace R and T by
   a paper and pens, respectively
   b paper and cartons, respectively
   c leather and magazine, respectively
   d paper and cotton, respectively

24. The things listed in column S tell us that
   a these are obtained from plants
   b plants are important for us
   c plants have a root and shoot system
   d Both (a) and (b)

25. Which one of these items is made up of more than one material?
   a Pen
   b Mug
   c Vest
   d Saree

26. Consider the statements given by three students.

Ujjawal There are over 600 muscles in our body and these muscles are classified as smooth muscles, special heart muscle and muscles attached to the bones.

Rudra These muscles often work in opposition. Through their coordination of relaxation and contraction, the muscles allow the arm to bend and straighten.

Riya When we are straightening our arm, the set of muscles on the upper side contracts while the other set on the lower side will relax.

Which of the above students is saying wrong?
   a Ujjawal
   b Riya
   c Rudra
   d Rudra and Riya

27. The brightness of an electric bulb depends on the amount of electrical energy converted into light energy. This electrical energy in turn depends on the amount of voltage (V) supplied.

The circuits shown below use identical bulbs which shine with equal brightness

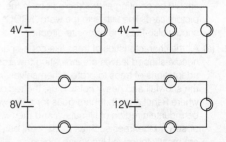

The circuits given in the options below also contains bulbs identical to those used in above circuits.

In which circuit do the bulbs shine as brightly as those in the circuits above?

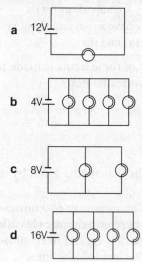

a   12V

b   4V

c   8V

d   16V

28. Geeta moves on a straight road from point A to point C. She takes 10 min to cover a certain distance AB and 20 min to cover the rest of distance BC. She then turns back and takes 20 min to cover the distance CB and 10 min to cover the rest of the distance to her starting point. She makes 4 rounds on the road in the same way. Her motion is

    a only rectilinear

    b only periodic

    c both rectilinear and periodic

    d neither rectilinear nor periodic

29. Observe the given below flow chart, there are some steps missing which are labelled as *P*, *Q* and *R*. Identify them.

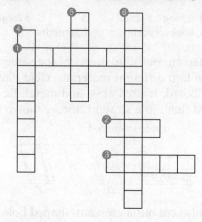

	P	Q	R
a	Butter	Milk	Cheese
b	Milk	Cheese	Butter
c	Milk	Cream	Butter
d	Cream	Milk	Cheese

30. Solve the crossword with the help of given clues.

Across

1. Aquatic animal, do not possess streamlined body.

2. Have long hairs on its body to prevent itself from the cold.

3. Plants respond to ....

Down

4. Do not possess gills and breathe in air through blowholes or nostrils.

5. Can stay both in water as well as land. They have webbed feet.

6. All living organisms commonly possess ....

Answers

9. (d) Group 1 involves cotton, jute and flax are plant products i.e. they are obtained from plant where as group 2 involves fur, leather and silk which are obtained from animals or insects.

10. (a) When sugar solution is heated, water evaporates, so only physical change takes place. However, when sugar is heated alone, first it loses water molecules and result in the formation of a new substance and turns black. So, it is a chemical change.

11. (c) An energy pyramid is a graphical structure of energy flow in a community. The energy flow occurs from bottom to up.

Producers (plants) bring energy from non-living sources. Animals that eat only plants are called herbivores and animals that eat other animals called carnivores.

12. (d) Wheat is the edible part of wheat plant, i.e. seed.

Sugar is obtained from sugarcane.

For preparing kheer, we need milk, rice and sugar.

Milk is obtained from cow, buffalo, goat. Meat is obtained from sheep, goat and chicken.

13. (d) The sun rises in the east. Hence, the shadow is cast towards the west. Since, the shadow of tree A lies in the west, the time should be around morning. The shadow of the tree is the shortest during noon which can be shown for tree B. The shadow of tree C lies in the east and the time should be around late afternoon to evening.

14. (c)

15. (c) Magnets should be kept in pairs with their unlike poles on the same side. Their ends must be shielded by metallic plates and they should be separated from each other using a piece of wood.

16. (c) A neither has definte volume nor definite shape, i.e. it is a gas e.g. helium. In case of B volume is definite but shape does not, so it is a liquid e.g. syrup. C is a solid like vase with definite shape and definite volume.

17. (b)

18. (a) As we know very well that the roots of a plant will move towards the earth because they are positively geotrophic and stem are negatively geotrophic. Thus, they will grow oppositely from the earth surface.

19. (c) Fertilisers enhance the growth of plants as observed from the observations of the table.

20. (c) Forearm and lower leg has 2 long bones. Wrist and ankle has several small bones. Palm and foot has 5 bones. Fingers and toe are composed of 3 large bones.

21. (d) Since, the question only asks that the crescent-shaped patch of light be formed on Sheet Y, we should concentrate on identifying the type of materials for Sheets W, X and Y. In order to have the bright crescent shape on sheet Y, Sheet X must be transparent while sheet Y must be opaque as it will prevent the light from passing through to reach Sheet Z. Moreover, Sheet W must be translucent allowing only the light to pass through the hole. Clear plastic sheet is chosen to be Sheet X as it is transparent while metal which is opaque is chosen to be Sheet Y. The frosted glass allows some light to pass through. Hence, it is placed at the back.

22. (b) Because all these things are made up of plastics.

23. (b) R = Paper, T = Cartons. As all the items are made up of paper.

24. (a) Because all the mentioned items are obtained from the plants.

25. (a)　　　　**26.** (b)　　　　**27.** (b)

28. (c)

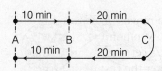

She is moving in rectilinear motion. Since, she repeats her walk on the same path which shows she possesses periodic motion also.

29. (c) Cow produces milk, from which cream is obtained. After processing, cream provides butter.

30.

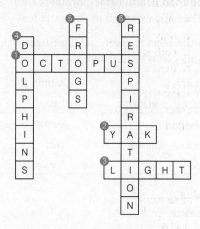

Practice Set ②

A Whole Content Based Test for Class 6th Science Olympiad

1. The underside of a leaf was studied under a microscope and tiny openings were seen as shown below. Which one of the following statements is true about the tiny openings?

- **a** They absorb sunlight
- **b** They take in water for the plant
- **c** They take in minerals for the plant
- **d** They allow oxygen to enter the leaf

2. Match the objects given in Column I with the materials given in Column II.

	Column I		Column II
A.	Surgical instruments	1.	Plastic
B.	Newspaper	2.	Animal product
C.	Electrical switches	3.	Steel
D.	Wool	4.	Plant product

Codes

	A	B	C	D
a	3	4	1	2
b	3	4	2	1
c	4	3	1	2
d	4	3	2	1

3. A few characteristic features of a plant are given below.
- I. Roots are much reduced in size.
- II. Stems are generally long and narrow.
- III. Stems possess air spaces.
- IV. Leaves are large and flat.
- V. They have waxy upper surfaces.

To which of these habitats does the plant belong?
- **a** Desert
- **b** Tropical rainforest
- **c** Water
- **d** Polar region

4. Rohit is standing near the wall in a dark room such that he is facing the mirror which is hung on the wall. When some light is put on him from a distance, X is observed in the mirror while Y is observed on the wall behind him. What is X and Y respectively?
- **a** Shadow, image
- **b** Image, shadow
- **c** Shadow, shadow
- **d** Image, image

5. Nishi took 2 shallow bowls of the same kind. She filled them with equal quantity of water and kept one of these bowls in the Sun and other in shade.

She observed less water in the bowl kept in Sun. What conclusion did she make after the experiment?
- **a** Rate of evaporation increases with increase in temperature
- **b** Rate of evaporation decreases with increase in temperature
- **c** Rate of evaporation is unaffected by temperature
- **d** None of the above

6. Consider the following changes:

X   Y

X and Y are
  a respectively irreversible and reversible changes
  b respectively reversible and irreversible changes
  c Both irreversible changes
  d Both reversible changes

7. We get energy from food. The following table illustrates the energy obtained from some food items and the amount of energy obtained by substituting these food items.

Food item	Energy (in kJ)	Substituted food item	Energy (in kJ)
Kachori, 1	190	Samosa, 1	103
Potato Vada, 1	118	Dahi Vada, 1	83
Chaat, 100 g	474	Bhel Puri, 100 g	182
Potato chips, 20 g	108	Peanuts (roasted) 1 tablespoon full	86

Which of the following pairs of food items shows the reduction in the energy values to the greatest extent?
  a Potato Vada—Dahi Vada
  b Potato Chips—Peanuts
  c Chaat—Bhel Puri
  d Kachori—Samosa

8. Which of the following statement hold true for the root system shown in the given figure?

  I. It is a fibrous root system.
  II. The branches that arise from the main root.
  III. It is a tap root system.
  IV. Example of this type of root.

System are pea, tulsi, radish, carrot and turnip.

Codes
  a I and II   b II and IV
  c III and IV   d II and III

9. The figure shows a water lily plant.

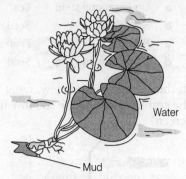

Water

Mud

What is the function of the roots?
  I. To absorb water.
  II. To absorb mineral salts.
  III. To hold the plant firmly to the soil.
  IV. To store food for the plant.

Codes
  a I and II
  b III and IV
  c I, II and III
  d I, II and IV

10. A piece of steel can be magnetised by stroking it with a magnet.

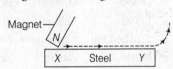

Magnet

N

X   Steel   Y

When the magnet is moved in the direction shown, which poles are produced at X and at Y?

	X	Y
a	North	North
b	North	South
c	South	North
d	South	South

11. Plants store excess sugar as starch in different plant parts. The classification structure below shows two different groups of plant parts.

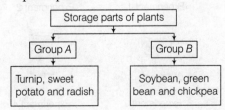

Storage parts of plants

Group A → Turnip, sweet potato and radish

Group B → Soybean, green bean and chickpea

Identify appropriate terms for group *A* and group *B*.

Codes

	Group *A*	Group *B*
a	Underground stem	Leaf
b	Root	Seed
c	Root	Fruit
d	Underground stem	Seed

12. In the set-up shown below, what would be the correct shape of the shadow formed on screen?

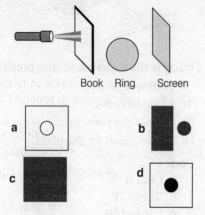

Book   Ring   Screen

13. Which of the following objects has a property that is incorrectly stated?

	Object	Material	Floats on water
a	Eraser	Rubber	Yes
b	Crushed foil	Aluminium	No
c	Bottle	Plastic	Yes
d	Bird house	Wood	Yes

14. Different amounts of 25°C water are added to four beakers. A thermometer is placed in each beaker and the beakers are set on hot plates. The time it takes the water to boil and the temperature of the water are shown in the picture below.

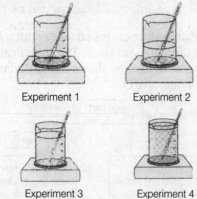

Experiment 1   Experiment 2

Experiment 3   Experiment 4

Time to boil	2.0 min	3.9 min	6.1 min	8.0 min
Boiling temperature	100°C	100°C	100°C	100°C

Which conclusion is supported by the data?

a The time to boil water is not affected by the amount of water

b The time to boil water is affected by the temperature at which water boils

c Water's boiling temperature is not affected by the amount of water

d Water's boiling temperature is affected by the time it takes water to boil

15. Identify *A*, *B*, *C*, and *D* in the following shown figure.

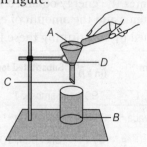

Select the correct option

	A	B	C	D
a	funnel	filter paper	filtrate	residue
b	funnel	residue	filtrate	filter paper
c	filter paper	funnel	residue	filtrate
d	filtrate	filter paper	funnel	residue

16. The live wire of an electric kettle becomes loose and touches the metal casing. Which of the following would occur next?

a Person touching it will get an electric shock

b Bubbles will form in the water

c Sparks will be seen

d The leakage of the current will be carried away by the earth wire

17. One day, when Seema was in Mumbai, she found that the water supplied to them is salty in taste. In order to get drinking water from it, she selected two techniques.

Could you guess what two techniques did she select?

a Evaporation and filtration

b Centrifuging and filtration

c Evaporation and distillation

d Sieving and decanting

18. Which of the following is a correct pair of the deficiency disease and its deficient nutrient?

	Deficiency disease	Deficient nutrient
a	Anaemia	Phosphorus
b	Goitre	Iodine
c	Cancer	Vitamin-C
d	Marasmus	Calcium

19. Observe the diagrams shown below carefully to form a magnet.

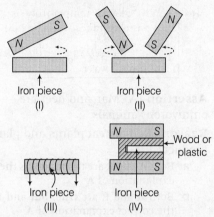

Which among them is not the correct method?

a I and II   b Only II
c I, II and III   d Only IV

20. The diagrams below show three closed circuits in which all the bulbs light up. The bulbs and batteries used in each circuit are the same.

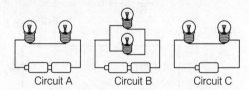

Arrange the circuits according to the brightness of the bulbs, beginning with the brightest.

a A, B, C   b C, A, B
c B, A, C   d C, B, A

21. Dinesh set-up an experiment shown below.

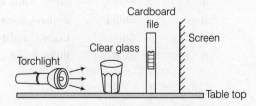

He placed two objects, a clear glass and a cardboard file, on the table in front of a torchlight. He then turned on the torchlight and the shadow was cast on the screen. Which of the following is the correct shadow produced on the screen?

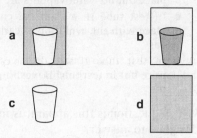

22. You might have observed the preparation of ghee from butter and cream at home. Which method(s) can be used to separate ghee from the residue?

I. Evaporation   II. Decantation
III. Filtration   IV. Churning

Which of the following combination is the correct answer?

a I and II   b II and III
c II and IV   d Only IV

23. Consider the given below statements.

I. It carries the essential substances like minerals and vitamins to the body cells.

II. It helps in removing waste material out of the body.

Which of the following is the best suitable term that can follow the above statements?

a Roughage
b Water
c Minerals
d Nutrients

24. Sohan took 2 mL lemon juice in two different test tubes and add 1 g of salt (common salt) in one test tube and 1 g washing soda in another.

The observation of Sohan is shown below.

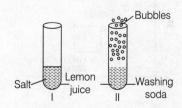

Which of the following is the correct reason for this observation?

a In test tube II, a chemical change takes place with the evolution of water vapours

b In test tube I, a chemical change takes place but no water vapours are formed

c In test tube II, a chemical change takes place with the evolution of carbon dioxide gas

d In test tube I, salt dissolves in lemon juice but in test tube II washing soda does not

25. Which question is this apparatus most likely designed to answer?

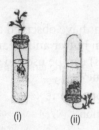

(i)   (ii)

a Does atmospheric pressure affect transpiration?

b Does gravity affect the direction of plant growth?

c Does turgor pressure affect the absorption of water?

d Does absorbed light increase the environmental temperature?

26. A stem was left in a beaker containing red coloured water. Which of the following options shows the correct inference about the colour of the leaves?

a
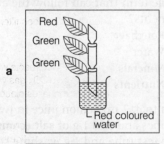

b
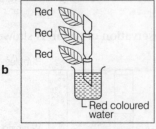

c
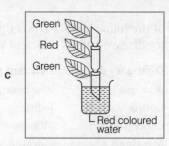

d
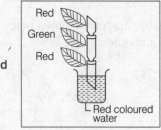

27. Assertion (A) Man and deer are omnivorous animals.

Reason (R) They eat plants and plants products.

a Both A and R are true and R is the correct explanation of A

b Both A and R are true, but and R is not the correct explanation of A

c A is true, but R is false

d Both A and R are false

28. The circuit diagram below consists of 5 bulbs A, B, C, D, and E and 3 switches X, Y and Z.

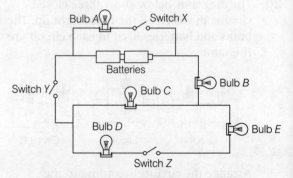

Which of the following shows the correct result when 1 of the switches is open and one of the bulbs is fused?

	Switch opened	Bulb that fused	Bulb(s) that remain lit
a	X	Bulb C	Bulbs D and E
b	Y	Bulb D	Bulbs A, B and C
c	Z	Bulb B	Bulbs C and E
d	X	Bulb E	Bulbs B and C

Practice Set 2

29. John used three metal bars of the same size to attract some thumbtacks. From the diagrams of his observation below, he can say that

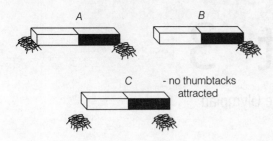

C — no thumbtacks attracted

a C is a strong magnet
b Only A and B are magnets
c B is a stronger magnet than A
d the thumbtacks have magnetic force

30. Consider the given state
Contraction of the 'B' pulls the 'A' during movement. Which of the following is placed at the place of A and B?

	A	B
a	Cartilages	Bone
b	Bones	Cartilages
c	Bones	Muscles
d	Muscles	Bones

Answers

1. (d) The structure shown in the figure is stomata, which allow gaseous exchange in plants.

2. (a) Surgical instruments are generally made up of steel because steel is resistant to corrosion and has good strength.
   Newspaper is made up of paper which is obtained from plants.
   Plastics are used to make electrical switches.
   Wool is obtained from sheep, an animal.

3. (b) In the tropical rainforest region planty of water remain present for plants. Thus due to the excess of water.

4. (b) A mirror forms an image, whereas a shadow is formed on the wall.

5. (a)

6. (d) Both the changes are reversible, i.e. can be converted into one another.

7. (c) The energy produced by 100 gm chaat is 474 kJ. Whereas 100 g bhel puri produces 132 kJ. Here the same quantity is producing variate amount of energy and a huge reduction of energy in comparison of other options.

8. (c) The given plant root is showing a tap root system as be usually can observe in carrot, turnip, radish, etc on which we can find small fibres around them.

9. (b)

10. (b) In single stroking, two opposite poles would be produced. The point on steel which the magnet last leaves will be in opposite polarity to that of magnet. Since, N-pole of magnet is stroking the steel, point Y will be S-pole.
    Point X will be N-pole as a magnet must have N and S-poles.

11. (b)

12. (c) Book is an opaque object so, it will block all the light rays incident on it. Hence, the shadow will be that of the book only, i.e. rectangular.

13. (a) Eraser shrinks in water.

14. (c) Water's boiling temperature is not affected by the amount of water.

15. (b)   16. (d)   17. (c)

18. (b) The deficiency of iodine causes the disease goitre. The deficiency of iron causes the disease anaemia.
    Cancer is not related to deficiency diseases. It is a degenerative type of disease.
    Marasmus is a disease occur due to the deficiency of protein in diet.

19. (d) In case of IV wood or plastic are non-magnetic materials rest all the figures depict magnetizing a magnetic material.

20. (c) Bulb in the parallel connection glow brightest. In case of circuit C both the bulbs are in series and connected to single battery. Hence, they will be least bright.

21. (d) Since cardboard file is an opaque object. So, no light will pass through it and the shadow will be that of the file.

22. (b) Ghee is first decanted and then filtered to remove associated impurities.

23. (b)

24. (c) Acid present in lemon juice reacts with mild base like washing soda to give CO_2 gas with common salt (neutral) no reaction takes place.

25. (b)

26. (b) Red water travels along with the xylem throughout the plant shown in figure b.

27. (c) Man and deer are omnivorous animals, as they eat both plants and animals.

28. (d)   29. (b)

30. (c) Contraction of the bones pulls the muscles during movement.

Practice Set ③

1. Consider the following information.

Plants do not move around in search of food and shelter. However, you can observe movements in plant when you touch the leaves of the *Mimosa* (touch-me-not) plant or in sunflower as it turns to face the sun.

Which conclusion can be best drawn from the above information?

a Plants show locomotion
b Plants respond to stimulus
c Plants can move their body parts
d Both b and c

2. Use the table below to answer the question

	Substances in centre			
Property	**W**	**X**	**Y**	**Z**
State	solid	solid	solid	liquid
Attracted to magnet	yes	no	no	yes
Dissolves in water	yes	no	yes	no
Colour	white	white	white	silver

Which substance shown in the table could be sugar?

a Substance *W*
b Substance *X*
c Substance *Y*
d Substance *Z*

3. Which of the following does not express a time interval?

a A day
b A second
c A school period
d Time of the first bell in the school

4. Study the classification chart given below.

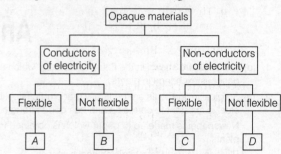

Which of the following correctly shows objects *A*, *B*, *C* and *D*?

	A	*B*	*C*	*D*
a	Nylon	Iron nail	Spectacle lens	Glass mug
b	Nylon	Aluminium foil	Carpet	Rubber ball
c	Copper wire	Steel spoon	Rubber ball	Spectacle lens
d	Copper wire	Iron nail	Metal spoon	Glass mug

5. Four students, Ravi, Ali, Shabina and Preeti were discussing about the habitats of various plants.

Ravi A banana plant has a green and soft stem. It is a herb.

Ali Strawberry is a climber plant with weak stems that cannot stand upright.

Shabina Maize, wheat and barley are plants with fibrous roots.

Preeti Stem, leaves, buds and flowers are included in the shoot system of the plant.

Which among these children made an incorrect statement?

a Ravi
b Ali
c Shabina
d Preeti

6. Rohit cannot be clearly seen when he stands behind the partition as shown below.

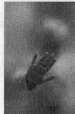

What according to you could be the reason?
- **a** The partition can reflect light
- **b** The partition is made of frosted glass
- **c** The partition allows most light to pass through
- **d** The partition is made of a material that does not allow light to pass through

7. Assertion (A) Breaking of a glass bowl is a chemical change.

Reason (R) Chemical changes are irreversible in nature.
- **a** Both A and R are true and R is the correct explanation of A
- **b** Both A and R are true but R is not the correct explanation of A
- **c** A is true but R is false
- **d** R is true but A is false

8. Derrick set-up an experiment to find out how long an ice cube takes to melt. He drew a graph to show the changes in the temperature of the melting ice cube.

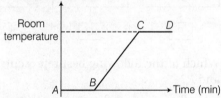

The ice cube had melted completely by point
- **a** A
- **b** B
- **c** C
- **d** D

9. The materials for making an object are chosen on the basis of properties of the materials and the purpose for which the object (item) is made. On the basis of her knowledge, Kavika made a few choices.
- I. She selected steel for making pan to cook food.
- II. She selected glass for making windowpane to look through.
- III. She selected plastic for making bucket to fill water.
- IV. She selected cotton cloth for making tumbler to drink water.

The correct choices made by her are
- **a** I and II
- **b** I, II and III
- **c** II, III and IV
- **d** Only II

10. Which of the following combination is/are correct?

	Types of consumer	Description	Example
I.	Herbivores	Eat plants only	Camel
II.	Carnivores	Eats both plant and animals	Wolf
III.	Omnivores	Eat animals only	Crow
IV.	Scavenger	Consume dead organisms only	Hyena

Codes
- **a** I and II
- **b** Only III
- **c** II and III
- **d** Only IV

11. In the diagram below, an object at A could be seen clearly if X was made of

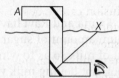

- **a** plastic
- **b** polished wood
- **c** clear glass
- **d** polished metal

12. Consider the following three situations:

Which of these show(s) a reversible change?
- **a** I and II
- **b** II and III
- **c** Only III
- **d** I, II and III

13. During swimming, which of the following movement is shown by a fish?

- **a** Muscles make the front part of the body curve to one side and the tail part towards the same side
- **b** Muscles make the front part of the body curve to one side and the tail part towards the opposite side.
- **c** Muscles make the whole body straight
- **d** All of the above

14. Consider the circuit diagram shown below.

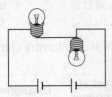

Which of the circuit below will have the same brightness as the above circuit?

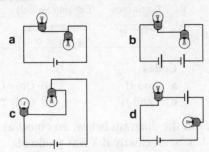

15. Sheela, Saima and Ravi have to dissolve maximum amount of sugar in the same amount of milk so as to win in a game. Ravi took hot boiling milk while Saima took ice cold milk. Sheela managed to get milk at room temperature. Whom do you think would win the game and why?

    a Sheela because solubility is maximum at room temperature.

    b Saima because solubility increases with decrease in temperature.

    c Ravi because solubility increases with increase in temperature.

    d No one as solubility is not affected by change in temperature.

16. There are four plants shown below. Which of them shows the best structural adaptation of leaves for protecting themselves from predators?

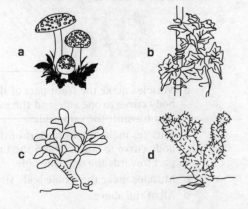

17. A piece of ribbon folded five times is placed along a 30 cm long measuring scale as shown in figure.

The length of the ribbon is between

    a 1.15 m - 1.25 m

    b 1.25 m - 1.35 m

    c 1.50 m - 1.60 m

    d 1.60 m - 1.70 m

18. **Assertion** (A) Water acts as an universal solvent.

    Reason (R) It has the capacity to freeze universally at zero degree celsius.

    Consider the above A and R, and choose the correct option.

    a Both A and R are true and R is the correct explanation of A

    b Both A and R are true, but R is not the correct explanation of A

    c A is true but R is false

    d Both A and R are false

19. Study the classification shown in diagram below and answer the question that follows.

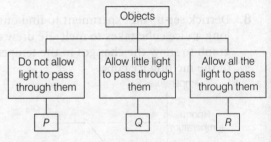

Which of the following best represents P, Q and R?

	P	Q	R
a	Wooden ruler	Air	Tracing paper
b	Tracing paper	Air	Wooden ruler
c	Air	Tracing paper	Wooden ruler
d	Wooden ruler	Tracing paper	Air

20. Manish's mother asked him, "What he would like to have in dinner?"
He replied following list of items, i.e.
aloo sabji, fruit, salad rice and roti with butter
Then, which of the essential nutrients is significantly absent in his dinner?

    a Proteins   **b** Carbohydrates

    c Fats   **d** Vitamins

Practice Set 3

21. The diagram below shows ammeter readings in a circuit. Which ammeter is showing a faulty reading?

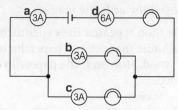

22. Which of the following graphs best represents the correct relationship between the rate of evaporation and humidity?

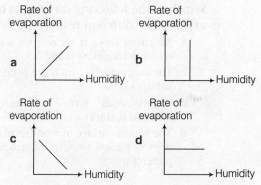

23. Rohit placed object *X* near a magnet and nothing happened. He then stroked it with a magnet in one direction many times and placed it near some iron filings. Which of the statements below is true?

    a Object *X* is a metal

    b Object *X* is a magnetic material

    c Object *X* is a temporary magnet

    d Object *X* will not attract the iron filings

24. The diagrams below show four different circuits.

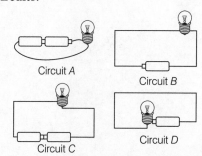

In which circuit(s) will the bulb light up?

    a Only *A*   **b** *B* and *C*

    c *A* and *D*   **d** *B*, *C* and *D*

25. Pallavi made paste of two food items *P* and *Q* each and put them in two test tubes. She added dilute iodine solution to food item *P*, while copper sulphate solution and caustic soda to food item *Q*. Which of the following combination is the correct result of her testing?

Codes

    a *P* contains starch and thus produce blue black colour

    b *Q* contains proteins and thus produce pink colour

    c *P* contains proteins and thus produce blue black colour

    d *Q* contains starch and thus produce pink colour

26. The flow chart given shows how some living things are classified.

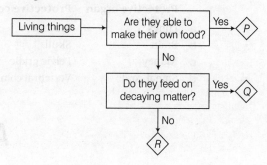

Identify *P*, *Q* and *R*.

	P	Q	R
a	Mouse	Mushroom	Mango
b	Grass	Mould	Frog
c	Mushroom	Grass	Mould
d	Fern	Grasshopper	Moss

27. A small compass is placed beside the middle of a bar magnet.

In which direction will be compass needle point?

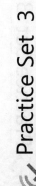

28. Observe the given flow chart.

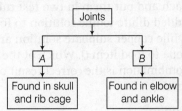

Identify the group in which 'knee' can be placed.

Codes

a *A*   b *B*

c Both *A* and *B*   d None of these

29. Which of the following is not a protective function of the endoskeleton?

Codes

	Protective organ	Protective covering
a	Lungs	Ribcage
b	Brain	Skull
c	Kidney	Pelvic gridle
d	Spinal cord	Vertebral column

30. Ruchi placed a paperclip on a glass plane and then placed a magnet 3 cm from the paperclip. She observed that the paperclip moved towards the magnet.

She then repeated the experiment with the same magnet and paperclip on a plank of wood. However, the paperclip did not move.

Which of the following statements best explains the different results?

a Magnetic force is weaker on a plank of wood than a glass plane

b The magnet in set-up *B* is weaker than in set up *A*

c Gravitational force is stronger on wooden surfaces

d The rough surface of wooden plank does not allow smooth movement of paperclip

Answers

1. *d*	2. *c*	3. *d*	4. *c*	5. *b*	6. *b*	7. *d*	8. *b*	9. *b*	10. *c*
11. *d*	12. *b*	13. *a*	14. *b*	15. *c*	16. *d*	17. *b*	18. *b*	19. *d*	20. *a*
21. *a*	22. *c*	23. *c*	24. *c*	25. *a*	26. *b*	27. *a*	28. *b*	29. *c*	30. *d*

Answer & Explanations

6

1 Food: Where does It Come From?

A. Introduction

1. c   2. c   3. b   4. d   5. b   6. d   7. a   8. b   9. b   10. d
11. d   12. c   13. c   14. d   15. b   16. c   17. d   18. c   19. c   20. d

B. Components of Food

1. a   2. a   3. b   4. b   5. b   6. d   7. b   8. d   9. c   10. d
11. b   12. b   13. d   14. d   15. b   16. c   17. a   18. b   19. b   20. a
21. d   22. c   23. d   24. c

2 Fibre to Fabric

1. d   2. c   3. d   4. b   5. c   6. c   7. a   8. c   9. b   10. c
11. d   12. d   13. c   14. a   15. c   16. b   17. c   18. b   19. a   20. a
21. a   22. b   23. b   24. b   25. a   26. b   27. c   28. d   29. b   30. c
31. c   32. b   33. c   34. c   35. c   36. b   37. b   38. a   39. d   40. b

3 Sorting and Separation of Materials into Groups

A. Sorting Material into groups

1. d   2. c   3. b   4. c   5. d   6. d   7. a   8. c   9. b   10. b
11. c   12. a   13. d   14. c   15. b   16. b   17. c   18. d   19. c   20. a
21. b   22. c   23. c   24. c   25. c   26. d   27. c   28. b   29. d   30. c
31. b   32. d   33. b   34. a   35. b   36. b   37. c   38. b

B. Separation of Substances

1. a   2. d   3. c   4. b   5. a   6. a   7. b   8. d   9. a   10. a
11. c   12. d   13. c   14. c   15. c   16. d   17. c   18. d   19. c   20. a
21. a   22. a   23. b   24. b   25. b   26. d   27. b   28. d   29. c   30. b
31. b   32. d

4 Changes Around Us

1. c   2. c   3. c   4. c   6 a   7. c   8. d   9. d   10. c   11. d
12. b   13. c   14. a   15. d   16. d   17. b   18. b   19. d   20. d   21. a
22. a   23. a   24. a   25. b   26. b   27. c   28. b   29. d   30. d   31. d
32. b   33. b   34. d   35. d

5 Getting to Know Plants

1. d   2. c   3. d   4. a   5. a   6. b   7. a   8. a   9. d   10. b
11. a   12. b   13. a   14. d   15. d   16. b   17. d   18. c   19. b   20. b
21. b   22. d   23. c   24. b   25. b   26. c   27. b   28. d   29. b   30. a
31. b   32. b   33. b   34. d   35. a   36. b   37. b   38. d   39. d   40. b
41. b   42. c   43. c   44. d   45. a   46. c   47. b

6 Body Movements

1. *d*	2. *a*	3. *c*	4. *b*	5. *c*	6. *d*	7. *b*	8. *a*	9. *b*	10. *c*
11. *b*	12. *a*	13. *b*	14. *d*	15. *a*	16. *a*	17. *c*	18. *b*	19. *b*	20. *d*
21. *d*	22. *b*	23. *a*	24. *a*	25. *a*	26. *c*	27. *a*	28. *b*	29. *b*	30. *b*
31. *d*	32. *b*	33. *b*	34. *c*	35. *d*	36. *c*				

7 The Living Organisms and Their Surroundings

1. *d*	2. *d*	3. *d*	4. *b*	5. *c*	6. *d*	7. *d*	8. *b*	9. *d*	10. *c*
11. *c*	12. *a*	13. *b*	14. *b*	15. *c*	16. *b*	17. *b*	18. *c*	19. *b*	20. *d*
21. *c*	22. *d*	23. *c*	24. *a*	25. *d*	26. *a*	27. *b*	28. *a*	29. *c*	30. *b*
31. *a*	32. *a*	33. *c*	34. *d*	35. *b*	36. *c*	37. *a*			

8 Motion and Measurement of Distance

A. Motion and Its Types

1. *c*	2. *b*	3. *c*	4. *b*	5. *b*	6. *b*	7. *b*	8. *d*	9. *b*	10. *c*
11. *d*	12. *a*	13. *a*							

B. Measurement

1. *c*	2. *c*	3. *b*	4. *b*	5. *a*	6. *d*	7. *c*	8. *c*	9. *c*	10. *b*
11. *b*	12. *d*	13. *a*	14. *b*	15. *d*	16. *a*	17. *c*	18. *c*		

9 Light: Shadow and Reflection

A. Light

1. *d*	2. *c*	3. *c*	4. *b*	5. *b*	6. *a*	7. *b*	8. *d*	9. *d*	10. *c*
11. *d*	12. *a*	13. *c*	14. *c*	15. *c*	16. *c*				

B. Shadow

1. *a*	2. *c*	3. *c*	4. *a*	5. *b*	6. *c*	7. *a*	8. *a*	9. *b*	10. *b*
11. *d*	12. *d*	13. *d*	14. *b*	15. *a*	16. *d*				

C. Reflection of Light

1. *c*	2. *b*	3. *c*	4. *d*	5. *b*	6. *b*	7. *d*	8. *a*	9. *b*	10. *c*
11. *d*	12. *a*	13. *d*							

10 Electricity and Circuit

A. Electric Current and Circuit

1. *d*	2. *a*	3. *b*	4. *b*	5. *b*	6. *d*	7. *a*	8. *c*	9. *b*	10. *d*
11. *c*	12. *d*	13. *b*	14. *a*	15. *c*	16. *a*				

B. Electrical Conductivity and Domestic Circuit

1. *c*	2. *b*	3. *c*	4. *b*	5. *d*	6. *b*	7. *c*	8. *c*	9. *a*	10. *b*
11. *d*	12. *c*	13. *a*	14. *b*	15. *c*	16. *b*				

11 Fun with Magnets

A. Properties of a Magnet

1. *b*	2. *d*	3. *d*	4. *b*	5. *c*	6. *a*	7. *b*	8. *a*	9. *b*	10. *a*
11. *a*	12. *b*	13. *d*	14. *a*						

B. Magnetic Materials and Applications

1. *d*	2. *c*	3. *b*	4. *b*	5. *b*	6. *b*	7. *a*	8. *d*	9. *b*	10. *c*
11. *a*	12. *d*	13. *d*							

12 Water

1. *c*	2. *c*	3. *c*	4. *a*	5. *c*	6. *d*	7. *c*	8. *a*	9. *a*	10. *b*
11. *b*	12. *b*	13. *d*	14. *d*	15. *c*	16. *d*	17. *c*	18. *b*	19. *a*	20. *a*
21. *c*	22. *c*	23. *b*	24. *b*	25. *a*					

13 Air

1. *d*	2. *d*	3. *a*	4. *d*	5. *b*	6. *b*	7. *a*	8. *c*	9. *b*	10. *c*
11. *c*	12. *c*	13. *b*	14. *d*	15. *c*	16. *b*	17. *a*	18. *d*	19. *b*	20. *b*
21. *b*	22. *b*	23. *d*	24. *b*	25. *d*	26. *b*	27. *a*	28. *b*	29. *b*	30. *b*
31. *c*	32. *a*	33. *a*	34. *c*	35. *b*	36. *a*				

1 Food: Where Does It Come From

A Introduction

1. Sanguivorous animals survive by sucking the blood of their hosts, e.g. female mosquitoes. These are external parasites. Herbivorous animals are adapted to eat plants, e.g. male mosquitoes.

3. Prey is an animal hunted or caught by another animal for food. In the figures badger (I) is a predator that naturally prey on other animals like wood mouse (II).

4. Lizard usually eats small creatures like snails, spiders, caterpillars, etc.
   Insects usually feed by tearing or pinching off plant parts or animal parts, e.g. ants, termites, beetles, etc.

5, 6. The edible parts of banana plant are stem, fruit and flower while the edible parts of pumpkin plant are leaves, fruit, seeds flowers and fleshy shell.

8. Elephant is a herbivorous animal. It eats only plants or plant products.
   Lizard is a carnivore. It eats only other animals.
   Crow is an omnivorous animal. It can eat both plants and animals.

12. Lion is a carnivore, squirrel is an omnivore, eagle is a scavenger and deer is a herbivore.

15. A food chain is a linear sequence of links in a food web. Food chain is biologically a sequence of who eats whom.
    Grass → Grasshopper → Rat → Snake → Hawk.

17. Scavenger is an animal that eat dead bodies of other animals. Crow, vulture, hyena, etc are the examples of scavengers.

18. Egg is itself an animal product, used as food.
    Almond is a dry nut whereas cashew is a nut.

B Components of Food

1. Oranges are particularly rich in soluble fibre but they also provide some insoluble fibre. They are also an excellent source of vitamin-C.

2. Sprouts are germinated seeds. They are tremendous source of digestive enzymes and are rich in amino acids, vitamins, proteins and fibre content.

6. Marasmus is a form of severe malnutrition characterised by energy deficiency. It mainly occur due to protein deficient diet. Phosphorus deficiency causes neurological diseases and musculo-skeletal dysfunction. Diseases like dental caries is caused when fluoride consumption is law. Muscle cramps, tetanus, etc are symptoms of magnesium deficiency.

8. Water soluble vitamins dissolve in water and are not stored by the body, e.g. vitamin-B and C. Whereas fat soluble vitamins dissolve in fat before they are absorbed in the blood stream to carry out their functions, e.g. Vitamin -A, D, E and K.

9. Dietary fibres or roughage is the indigestable portion of food derived from plants. The consumption of foods high in fibre have been found to reduce appetite, e.g. whole grains, fruits and vegetables.

14. Minerals and vitamins are needed in small quantities. They are very important for normal functioning of the body.

15. After step IV, the crushed seed are taken out from the paper and the paper will be observed under sunlight. This paper will show bright and translucent spots, which shows the presence of fat.

24.

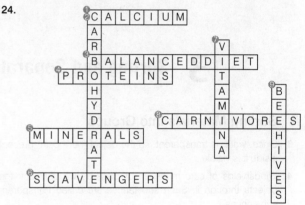

2 Fibre to Fabric

3. In the given option, (a) is Angora goat, (b) is common goat, (c) is yak and (d) is sheep, where sheep is the common source used for wool production in India.

4. Nylon is a man-made or synthetic fibre, made up of two chemicals, i.e. dichloride and diaminohexane. These two chemicals are required in the ratio of 2 : 5.

5. The tool shown in the figure is used for carding. Carding is a process used for disentangling and cleaning of wool.

6. Spinning is a process, in which the long woollen fibres are spun into thick yarns and reeling is a process of taking out silk from cocoons.

7. Silkworms feed on mulberry leaves. Silk production is indirectly dependent on plants.

17. Silk fibres are natural protein fibres. The protein fibre of silk is composed mainly of fibroin.

Reeling is a process involved in its production. It is defined as the process of taking out silk from cocoons.

The rearing of silkworms for obtaining silk is called sericulture.

20. The flow chart shown in the question is a sequential representation of silk production.

22. In group I, leather is an exception. It is a durable and flexible material obtained from cows, goats, pigs and sheep. It is not fibrous in nature.

In group II, water absorption is an exception to the properties of nylon.

37. Pashmina shawls are the famous product of Jammu and Kashmir. It is formed by the Angora wool obtained from Angora goat.

39. Llama and Alpaca are the animals that are used in wool production. They are mainly found in South America.

Woollen fibres are processed to obtain woollen yarn.

40.

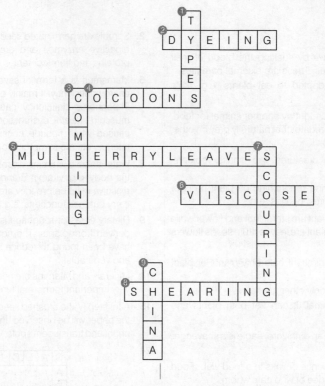

3 Sorting and Separation of Materials into Groups

A Sorting Materials into Groups

3. Since, water is transparent, so the object (here coin) present inside it is visible.

4. Windshields of cars made up of glass as we can look the objects through it. Such substances are called transparent substances.

5. Liquids have definite volume but their shape is not definite. They take the shape of the vessel in which they are placed. They are non-compressible.

6. P = Opaque, Q = Translucent, R = sand, S = oily paper.

8. As it is translucent.

9. The given things are non-living and translucent.

11. Copper is a good conductor of electricity.

12. Wooden and plastic rulers float while that of metal being heavier sinks.

13. Plastic and steel both can be used in a safety pin. As the designs attached with them are made up of plastics.

15. I to V all can be made up of metals but last two do not.

18. As honey is miscible with water.

19. P = transparent, Q = sink, R = lustrous, S = water.

20. As one can see through them.

21. For making a boat, the suitable material is that which is waterproof and can float over water.

22. X = Glass, Y = Rubber, Z = Metal

23. Because through opaque materials, one cannot see.

24. Glass bowl and steel spoon both will shine.

26. Stone is opaque while glass is transparent.

27. Tea cups may be of glass or plastic or China clay. Gas cylinder and pressure cooker are always metallic.

28. Pulses take the shape of the container in which these are placed but the shape of indivisible grain does not change. So, these are included in the category of solid substance.

Liquids have no definite shape. They generally take the shape of the container in which these are placed.

29. As increases in its length is minimum.

30. This experiment is done to show the effect of different materials on the time required to melt the all ice-cubes.

31. Because copper is very ductile, even more ductile as compared to iron, so generally used for making wires.

Note: Ductility is the property of a material to convert into wires.

32. A = Sugar, B = Gel, C = Oil, D = Glass, E = Chalk, F = Plastic lunch box.

33. The experiment suggests that the order of thermal conductivity of given materials is

Glass rod < Brass rod < Aluminium rod < Copper rod
(almost non-conducts)

35.

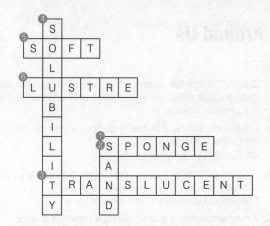

36. For storing items by a shopkeeper, the material must be transparent, so that the buyers can easily see the items placed in them.

37. For making buckets, the material should hard and insoluble. Further, it should be opaque and non-combustible.

38. As it is hard, non-transparent, non-combustible and completely miscible with water.

Ⓑ Separation of Substances

3. Lassi is prepared by churning.

8. Wheat being heavier is separated from lighter husk by winnowing.

9. Since, oil and water are immiscible liquids, so, they form separate layers. Oil being lighter remain in the upper layer.

12. Because of ice cold water, the outer surface of glass also become cool and the atmospheric water vapour when comes in contact of it, condenses in the form of droplets of water.

13. P = threshed, Q = winnowed, R = handpicked, S = sieved.

14. Because both are magnetic in nature.

15. Sand, chalk powder and saw dust are insoluble in water.

17. Decantation is done after sedimentation. All other statements are true.

18. Because winnowing is used to separate heavier components from the lighter one or the components that differ in their weights.

19. Evaporation is the process of spontaneous conversion of surface water into its vapour form at any temperature. When these water comes in contact of plastic bottle, they get condensed and again converted into water droplets.

20. Separating funnel is used to separate oil from water.
All other given statements are true.

21. P = Sublimation (because only naphthalene sublimes, i.e. converted directly into gaseous form from its solid state among the given).

Q = Magnetic separation (as iron is magnetic while others are not)

R = Filtration (because sand is immiscible with water.

S = Evaporation (because salt is obtained from salt solution by this method).

22. In case of suspension, the particles are large enough and hence, visible to naked eyes.
After keeping for a long period, the larger particles settle down and form sediment.
Without adding solute, the pure liquid component is called solvent. However, a mixture of solute and solvent is called solution.

23. By separation techniques, two or more different but useful components can be separated. Further, it is helpful in obtaining a pure substance from a sample by removing undesirable and useless components.

24. Evaporation is used to get back solid copper sulphate as all the water is lost during this technique.

25. P and Q are heavy but R is light, so winnowing help in separation of P and Q from R.
Q is magnetic but P not, so by magnetic separation, P and Q are separated.

26. First of all, she has to do filtration to remove sand. After that, she use separating funnel to separate oil from salt solution.
The salt from salt solution is separated by evaporation.

27. Oil mixed in water - Decantation. Iron powder (magnetic) mixed with flour (non-magnetic) - magnet.
Salt mixed with water - evaporation.
Lady's finger mixed with French beans - Handpicking.
Rice flour mixed with kidney beans - Sieving.

28. Winnowing is used to separate heavier substances from the lighter one and precipitation is the process of separation of a solid from a liquid mixture, when some reagent is added.
On heating, the solubility of a solid in liquid increases, i.e. a saturated solution becomes unsaturated and thus, more salt can be dissolved.

29. C is separated by filtration, so it must be immiscible with water, i.e. should be saw dust or sand. B and A are separated by distillation (boiling followed by condensation), so A should be completely miscible with B.
Thus, A = sugar and B = water.

31. P = condensation (conversion of vapours into water liquid by cooling them)
Q = Evaporation
R = Melting

32. Since, P remains in the China dish, so it is salt (the solid component) and thus, Q is water.
Salt from water is separated by evaporation.

④ Changes Around Us

1. Stretching of rubber band and dissolving of salt in water are reversible process. The remaining processes are irreversible.

3. Energy, colour, temperature, chemical composition all change during a chemical change.

4. Rolling of chapatti is a physical change (i.e. does not result in the formation of a new substance), so it can be reversed. But baking it result in the formation of some new compounds, so this change cannot be reversed.

5. Coal, Stone, Key, Pencil, Leaf.

6. Because water vapours when comes in contact of metal plate, condense there and appear as water droplets.

7. When POP is mixed with water, it forms a hard mass, called gypsum, which has a composition different from the POP. So, reconstruction is not possible.

8. Because on heating, the metals expand and on cooling, they again contract to regain their shape.

9. Earthquake is undesirable as well as irreversible change.

11. For boiling and melting, energy is required whereas in case of freezing, the stored energy is released, so, it is an exothermic process.

12. The changes shown are physical and reversible changes respectively. Because in first figure, the chemical composition remains unaffected and in latter figure, the spring regains its original shape.

13. The changes that occur at a regular interval are called periodic changes. They may be very slow to very fast. All the given phenomena are the examples of such changes.

14. P → Q is a reversible change (as no new substance is formed).
    Q → R is an irreversible change as the fabric (cloth) gets converted into black ash (a new substance).

15. Iron is more reactive than copper and hence, replace sulphate from copper sulphate (blue vitriol) solution.
    Change in chemical composition suggests that it is a chemical and irreversible change.

16. Both freezing of water and breaking of brick are the examples of physical changes as the chemical composition of substance remains the same before and after the change. Freezing although is a reversible change but breaking of brick is an irreversible change.

17. Formation of curd from milk is an irreversible chemical change because the chemical composition of curd and milk is different.

18. Except hardening of cement (which is a chemical change) all others are reversible changes.

19. P = red hot, Q = soft, R = cooling, S = hard

22. A = reversible changes
    B = irreversible changes, not chemical or temporary as breaking of brick is a physical change.

24. Tsunami is a natural change and souring of milk is an undesirable change. Glowing of electric lamp is a physical change.

Burning of candle involves both physical as well chemical changes as burning of wax is a chemical change while its melting is a physical change.

25. Explosion occurs with the evolution of energy so, it is an exothermic process.
    Remaining two statements are true.

26. Rusting of iron is a slow irreversible change and chemical changes are generally irreversible in nature.
    Remaining two answers were correct.

27. A new substance is formed during a chemical change.
    Remaining statements are true.

28. Magnetisation is a physical change. It is a temporary and reversible change.

29. Physical changes affect the physical properties like colour, state, etc.
    Rusting of iron is a slow process.
    Other statements are true.

30. Baking results in the change in composition. So, it is irreversible in nature.
    While making of clay pot is a reversible change.
    Energy is required for both the processes.

31. P → Q = Physical
    Q → R = Chemical
    R → S = Physical

32. Reversible changes – (i), (iii), (iv), (v), (vi)
    Irreversible changes – (ii), (vii), (viii)

36.

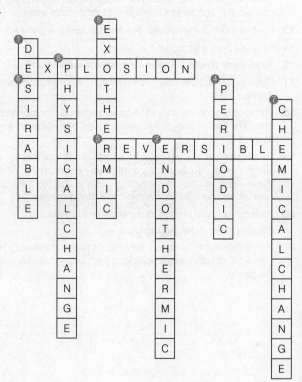

2. Green plants absorb light energy using chlorophyll present in their leaves. Using this energy, carbon dioxide react with water to make sugar or carbohydrate called glucose. The glucose is used in respiration or converted into starch and stored. Oxygen is produced as a by-product.

11. Grass shows parallel venation and so, it has fibrous roots. Parallel venation refers to a pattern in which the veins of a leaf run parallel to each other and perpendicular to primary vein.

16. The figure shows the process of transpiration. Transpiration is evaporation of water from plant leaves.

17. Shrub is small to medium-sized woody plant.
Herb is a flowering plant whose stem above ground does not become woody.
A tree is a tall plant with a trunk and branches made of wood.

19. Reticulation venation is observed in *B* and *C*. It is of two types, i.e. unicostate/pinnate *B* and multicostate/palmate type *D*. It refers to a pattern of veins, in which veins are branched repeatedly to form a network on the leaf lamina.

20. Xylem is a vascular tissue, which is involved in the upward movement of water, i.e. from roots to leaves in plant.

21. *Cuscuta* is a parasitic plant.
Monotropa is a saprophytic non-green plant.
Pitcher plant is an insectivorous plant.
Lichen on pine tree is an example of symbiotic plant.

24. Plants are multicellular in nature. They have more than one cell. They are autotrophic as they can make their own food by the process of photosynthesis.

31. Venus fly-trap is an insectivorous plant and *Cuscuta* is a parasitic plant.

33. Humidity means the moisture content of the air. The higher the humidity, the less water will evaporate from the leaves. This is because the diffusion gradient from the water between the air spaces inside the leaf and the wet air outside it is less. Thus, transpiration decreases as humidity increases.

42. Oxygen is produced or evolved during the process of photosynthesis.
Carbohydrate (glucose) is a product formed during photosynthesis.

44. The longitudinal and transverse section of ovary, i.e. lowermost swollen part of pistil shows ovule. It is a structure that gives rise to and contains the female reproductive cells.

48.

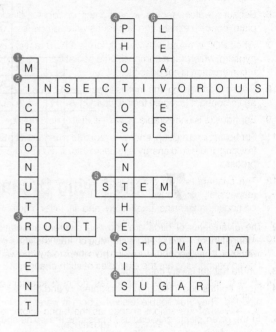

2. *X* denotes the pelvic girdle. It helps us in walking, running, standing and sitting. It supports the weight of our body when we stand, sit and helps in movement of the legs.

4. Bones give shape to our body. They support the surrounding muscles, connective tissues, etc and also provide protection to the major organs.
Muscles attach to bones, allowing them to move in conjunction with one another.

6. Ball and socket, pivot and hinge are the joints found in our body. Sternum or breast bone is the strong, flat dagger-shaped bone.

7. There are twenty two bones that make up the skull.
Hip bone is formed by the fusion of three bones.

8. Ribs are composed of 24 bones arranged in 12 pairs.
Vertebral column is made up of 26 serially arranged units called vertebrae.

12. *X* is coccyx. It is also referred to as tail bone and consists of 4 bones that fuse together as one grows up. It can variably consist of 5 or 3 bones as well. It is a regnant of a vestigial tail in all tailless primates.

13. Ball and socket joints are movable joints that allow the greatest freedom of movement. In these joints, the round head of one fits into the hollow, cup-shaped socket of another.
Hinge joint is also a movable joint. It works like a door hinge or penknife. In this, slightly bulging surface of one bone fits into the slightly depressed surface of another bone. Thus, allowing movement only in one direction.

16. The boy in the figure is using shoulders for lifting his hands. The human shoulder is composed of three bones, i.e. clavicle (collar bone), the scapula (shoulder blade) and the humerus (upper arm bone).

20. The doctor observed swelling and took an X-ray of the ankle. X-ray images confirm injuries/fracture in bones.

22. A snake forms loops in its body while slithering. Each loop of the snake gives it a forward push by pressing against the ground. The snake with a large number of loops moves much faster than the snake with less number of loops. Thus, snake '*A*' will move faster than snake '*B*'.

23. Kangaroo can jump or hop as well as walk but can not slither.

25. The figure A shows the hinge joint in a machine which seems to be similar to the hinge joint found in the elbow between humerus and ulna.

29. The outer part of the ear is not derived from the internal bone structures. The outer ear is made up of cartilage not bone.

32. Earthworms move by alternate extension and contraction of the body using muscles. Tiny bristles on the underside of the body help in gripping the ground.

36. The elbow has a hinge joint, that allows movement of bones in only one direction.

37.

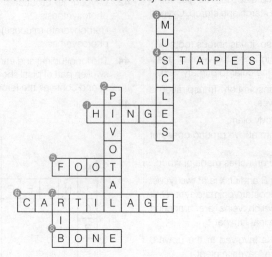

7 The Living Organisms and Their Surroundings

2. The given feets of birds are showing different adaptations, amongst them, A feet of bird is showing characteristics of good swimmer. It has webbed feet which help them to swim in water.

3. Tundra habitat is very cold habitat.

4. Frogs comes under the amphibian category and they are cold blooded. They are capable to survive both in water and land.

5. In the given plants only cactus D possess the spine-shaped leaves which helps it to protect itself from the predators.

6. The camel has long legs which help to keep its body away from the hot sand in the desert.

7. Xerocoles are terrestrial animals which can tolerate extremely dry conditions and pass long periods without water, e.g. camels.

12. Streamlined body is generally found in fishes, which help them to float easily inside water.

15. Water spider and water beetle do not possess gills or other special organ to breath inside the water. But they are well adapted to trap air with their body parts for breathing and thus, inside the water they can stay for a long time by utilising the traped amount of air.

25. The desert plants lose very little water through transpiration, as the leaves are either absent, very small or modified into spines. Desert plants mostly have long roots to absorb water from a larger area.

26. In a desert, the weather remain very hot due to which the body sweats out large amount of H_2O. Thus, loss of water from the body will result in small amount of urine and concentrated urine during excretion.

27. Camel stores fat in the hump(s), not water. This help it to survive long periods without food and water.

30. The birds A and C are correctly matched with their beak functions.

Bird A is showing a broad and strong beak which can easily scoop fish, out of the water and bird B is showing a long and narrow beak which is suitable to draw nectar easily from the flowers.

31. The pie chart is showing the rate of reproduction of frog and mosquitoes in a given time period. The resultant observation is that the frogs take more time to develop from an egg to adult. Thus, it is possible that in the time taken by frogs to develop, the mosquitoes will be more as they require very less time period in comparison to frogs.

Also, the pie graph tell that the food relationship between the frog and the mosquito is balanced.

34. In the fig, A shows a fish that breaths through gills. B is insect that has air tubes (trachae) for breathing and C is frog that breathes as adult through lungs.

35. In India, temperatures typically ranges from −2 to 40°C.

38.

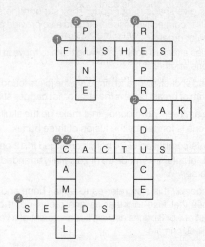

8 Motion and Measurement of Distance

A Motion and its Types

1. Because rifling the bullet also possess rotational motion along with rectilinear motion.

2. When the string is plucked it undergoes vibratory motion which is periodic in nature.

3. An artificial satellite moves around the earth in a circular path in periodic motion.

6. Motion of a swing is periodic.

7. All the hands of a watch are in periodic motion. In rotational motion, object spins on its own axis.

8. The wheel of a bicycle possess circular motion whereas the bicycle as a whole is in rectilinear motion. The motion of earth around the sun is a combination of rotational and revolutional motion. The pendulum of a pendulum clock is in periodic motion whereas the needles of the clock are in circulatory motion.

9. I. Motion II. Rectilinear III. Circular IV. Periodic V. Rotational

14.

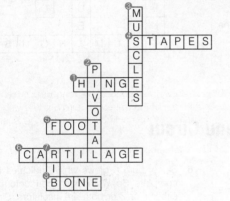

B Measurement

2. Number of divisions $= \dfrac{1\,m \times 1000}{0.1\,m} = 10000$

3. Total distance travelled in 7 h = (292 + 400) km = 692 km
$$= 692\,km$$

4. Length of each foot step = 30 cm
   Length of classroom = 30 × 20 = 600 cm
   Breadth of classroom = 30 × 15 = 450 cm

5. Number of coins = 10
   Total length = 2.9 − 0.9 = 2 cm = 20 mm
   Thickness of one coin $= \dfrac{20}{10} = 2\,mm$

7. 0.2 m = 0.2 × 100 = 20 cm

8. Length of stick A = 2.6 − 0.3 = 2.3 cm
   Length of stick B = 6.0 − 3.5 = 2.5 cm
   Length of stick C = 10.4 − 7 = 3.4 cm
   Length of stick D = 14.4 − 10.7 = 3.7 cm

9.

10. Length of micro SD card = 5.9 − 4.6
$$= 1.3\,cm = 1.3 \times 10$$
$$= 13\,mm$$

13. I. Unit   II. Cubit   III. Hand span   IV. 1000000   V. Foot

17. To measure the length of a curved line, scale and thread are used.

18. Required area = (10 × 2) + (2 × 2) + (2 × 6)
$$= 20 + 4 + 12 = 36\,cm\,sq$$

9 Light: Shadows and Reflections

A Light

1. Since, light propagates in straight line so, student A, B and C cannot see through the bent pipe. Only student D will be able to see the candle flame clearly from the straight pipe.

2. The small holes between the clusters of leaves act like pinholes and light rays of sun passes through these pinholes to form bright circular images of sun on the ground.

3. Translucent objects are the one through which only partial light passes. Transparent objects allow all the light rays to pass through them and opaque objects do not allow any light to pass through them.

4. Pinhole images are real and inverted. Moreover, sun is the source of light here, so, incident rays are the one coming from the sun and reflected rays are the one which are reflected from the person.

6. Mirror is a perfect reflector and hence an opaque object. Frosted glass allows some light to pass through it and hence a translucent object.

7. Pinhole images are real and inverted.

8. Distance of image of eye behind the mirror = 15 cm
   Distance of bird from the mirror = 100 + 15 = 115 cm
   Distance of bird from the image of her eye = (15 + 115) cm
$$= 130\,cm$$

13. Since, transparent glass allow all the light to pass through them hence window panes are generally made of transparent glass.

15. The luminous objects present in the figure are sun, lamp and television.

16. Boy, chair and table are non-luminous objects. Television is luminous object.

B Shadow

1. Any source of light can be used to produce a shadow whether it is sun or any man-made source of light like electric bulb.

2. None of the side of a shoe box is circular hence circular shadow can never be formed using it.

3. The shape and size of a shadow varies as per the alignment of source of light with respect to the object.

4. Frosted glass allows some of the light rays to pass through it hence colour of the shadow will be less darker as compared to the shadow cast by wooden box which being opaque does not allow any light to pass through it.

5. The length of his shadow depends on how far he is from the lamp. The further he is away from the lamp, the longer will be the shadow. The shortest shadow will be when he is just below the lamp i.e. at C.

6. Since, the shadow in option (c) is shortest so, it reveals that it is formed in afternoon time.

7. Shadow is formed when an object does not allow light to pass through it.

8. In figure (II) a pinhole image is formed.

9. The correct statement is that the incident angle is smaller in the morning which makes the shadows longer as light incident on it is coming obliquely.

12. Shadows are formed by an object obstructs the light to pass through them. The shadows are formed on the same side of the object.

13. Smaller sources of light create darker shadows. So, a candle or an electric bulb will form much sharper shadows than fluorescent tube-lights.

15. The darker portion is umbra and lighter portion of a shadow is penumbra.

C Reflection of Light

1. Smooth and polished surfaces cause regular reflection which produce clear images.

2. Red and yellow combine to form orange colour. So, the image of the transparent beaker will be orange.

3. A plane mirror always forms laterally inverted images.

4. Light rays reflected through the mirror forms an image at B on the screen.

5. Light rays undergo multiple reflections from each mirror in a periscope, so as to see a distant object.

6. Images formed by reflection of light can be real as well as virtual.

8. Regular reflection from smooth and polished surfaces causes glare in our eyes. Mirror helps to change the direction of light falling on it.

10. Incident rays are the one which are coming from the object towards the mirror and reflected rays are the rays which are bounced back from the mirror into our eyes.

14.

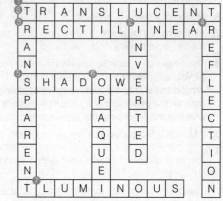

10 Electricity and Circut

A Electric Current and Circuit

1. When the switch is ON, circuit is complete and electric current will flow immediately. So, all the bulbs glow together.

2. In case of P, two cells are connected in series to form a battery so, large current can be drawn for the single bulb. So, the bulb in circuit P will glow brightest.

3. Current always flows from positive to negative terminal. In case of dry cell, the flattened disc is the negative terminal.

7. If both the terminals of a dry cell are connected to each other directly, then the wires get warm and circuit will get short which can cause injuries.

8. In case of circuit (II) both the terminals of cell are connected to single terminal only so, the circuit is not complete.

15. In case of a fused bulb, the filament is broken hence circuit is not complete and no current will flow.

B Electrical Conductivity and Domestic Circuits

1. Since plastic is an insulator so, no current will pass through it.

2. Wood and rubber are insulators. In options (a) and (c) one side is conducting and other side is insulating so, current will not flow through it. In option (c), both sides are insulating.

3. For bell C circuit is not complete so, Y must be an insulator.

4. Since, connecting B and C together does not light up the tester and connecting B and F together also showing the same result so, B must be an insulator hence, option (b) is correct.

5. A pencil lead is made up of graphite which is a good conductor of electricity.

6. Since, bulb A glows which indicates its circuit is complete. So, W and X are conductors. For bulb B either Y or Z or both are insulators. Since, bulb C glows which implies Y is also a conductor. Bulb D is connected to Z, Y and W and still does not glow so, either of them is an insulator. From the above observations we get to know that only Z is an insulator and rest all are conductors.

7. In case of option (c) fan, bulbs and generator all are in parallel connection along with separate switches.

12. Conductors are the materials which allow electric current to pass through them.

17.

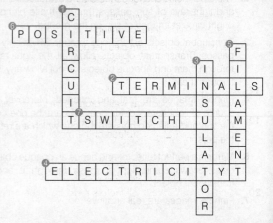

⑪ Fun with Magnets

Ⓐ A Properties of a Magnet

1. Each piece of broken bar magnet acts as a complete bar magnet with their own north pole and south pole.

2. Like poles of two magnets always repel each other and unlike poles always attract each other. So, car 1 and 2 will come closer whereas 3 and 4 will move away from each other.

3. For a single stroke, two opposite poles would be produced. The point of iron nail on which the magnet last leanes will be in opposite polarity of that of magnet.
   In the given case S-pole of magnet is stroking. So, point D will be N-pole.

4. Repulsion is the sure test of magnetism and not attraction.

5. A freely suspended magnet always align itself in geographical north-south direction. So, B is correct. Also, magnetic field of a magnet is strongest and equal at its pole. So, C is correct and A is incorrect.

11. South pole of freely suspended magnet is attracted by earth's north pole and north pole of the magnet is attracted by earth's south pole.

12. A magnet can be demagnetised by hammering, heating or dropping it from a height.

14. Since I attracts maximum iron filings at its poles so, it is the strongest magnet.

Ⓑ Magnetic Materials and Applications

1. Since cobalt and iron are magnetic materials. So, they can be separated from other metals using a magnet.

3. Steel is a non-magnetic material. It can be made magnetic either by passing current or by rubbing with a magnet in a regular fashion.

4. As per the observation N-pole of magnet X is facing towards N-pole of magnet Y. S-pole of magnet X is facing towards N-pole of magnet Z. N-pole of magnet Y is facing towards N-pole of magnet Z. So, magnet X will repel magnet Y and attract magnet Z. Magnet Y will repel both magnet X as well as magnet Z.

5. Steel will form a permanent magnet and not an electromagnet.

7. Repulsion is the sure test to check magnetism. Bar P and Bar R were pushed which implies they are magnets. Bar Q is not affected so, it must be some non-magnetic material like glass. Bar R is only pulled which implies it is some magnetic material like iron.

11. When the switch of door bell is pressed then circuit is setup and current starts to flow through the electromagnet. When the switch is left then circuit breaks and magnetism is lost.

12. Steel is a non-magnetic material whereas iron and nickel are magnetic materials.

14.

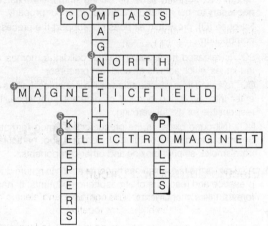

⑫ Water

3. A. Melting (ice melts with increase in temperature to form water).
   B. Evaporation (change of liquid state to a gaseous state, i.e water evaporates to form water vapours).
   C. Condensation (conversion of vapour or gas to liquid)
   D. Freezing (water changes to a solid form at 0°C).

5. Denim jeans is a heavy cloth. It retains large amount of water and take longest time for drying.

7. The fishes in B aquarium dies because boiled water is devoid of oxygen. Gas solubility increases with decreasing temperature (colder water holds more oxygen).

12. Apple chunks have some liquid retained in them which on heating, evaporate and appear as water droplets on the cling wrap.

13. **Set-up A** The water vapour from the surrounding air comes into contact with the cool surface of the metal lid and sides of the beaker.
    Set-up B The water vapour from the hot water in the beaker comes into contact with the cool surface of the metal lid.

20. To conduct a fair test, all factors must be same except for the temperature of the water.

21. Sea water contains a large amount of NaCl in it which changes the taste of the pure water, i.e. makes it salty in taste.
    Hence, sea water is not fit for drinking.
    River and lake water are the source of fresh water. Their water is fit for drinking.
    The component present in beaker B is water which can easily boils at 100°C.

27.

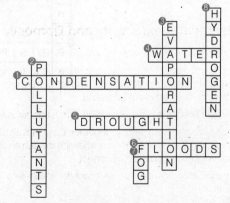

13 Air

1. Oxygen replaces I in the statements. Air is made up of nearly 78% nitrogen, 21% oxygen, 0.9% argon, 0.04% water vapour and 0.03% carbon dioxide. The presence of oxygen is essential for survival of living organisms. It is utilised by us in various metabolic processes for energy.

3. Stratosphere is the layer between tropopause and stratopause. It covers the distance of about 45 km above the tropopause. It contains ozone layer (O_3 layer) which protects the life on earth.

5. Oxygen (A) constitutes around 21% of total composition of air.
   Nitrogen (B) is about nearly 78% in air.
   Carbon dioxide, rare gases (argon, etc.) and water vapour constitute about 1% of air. Carbon dioxide is required for photosynthesis.

7. CO_2 (P) is a greenhouse gas. It leads to global warming (increase in the temperature of earth).
   Oxygen (S) is inhaled by us during respiration. As, it is necessary for our metabolic activities to occur properly.
   Nitrogen (Q), present in air does not support the process of combustion.

8. SO_2 is released from power plants, buildings, homes and industries which acts as an acid rain precursor.
   CO_2 released from various sources like industries, homes etc. enter into air during burning of different substance. It is responsible for global warming.
   NO_x (Nitrogen oxide) is the precursor for smog formation. Smog is a kind of air pollutant. It contains soot particulates from smoke, sulphur dioxide and other components.

11. Acid rain is the rain which has become acidic in nature due to presence and reactions of atmospheric pollutants. It harms forests, lakes, monuments, buildings, etc.

12. The gas stove usually uses fuels like natural gas or LPG, fuel oil, kerosene, wood or coal which on burning release number of gases in small quantities and from these gases NO_2 is released in maximum quantity.

14. Pure water is colourless, odourless, tasteless and transparent liquid.

16. Global warming leads to increased evaporation and precipitation due to increased level of temperature, which falls as increased snow in winter.

21. The petroleum jelly which gets maximum dust particles, shows the most polluted site.

24. Stratosphere covers the distance of about 45 km above the tropopause.
    Thermosphere covers the large part of the earth atmosphere, which is about 120 km above the mesopause.

25. The air becomes thinner with altitude. Hence, as we go up, O_2 decreases. Windmill uses the power of wind to generate electricity. Higher the temperature, lower is the solubility of air in water.

26. Oxygen present in air is necessary for the process of combustion.

28. Earthworm in container B will stay alive because the top of the container allow the gaseous exchange, as it has holes in it.

30. Photochemical smog does not involve SO_2 while winter smog does not involve NO_x.

33. The candle with the glass tumbler inverted over it went off after sometime because the oxygen present in the glass tumbler was used up. As O_2 is a supporter of combustion in its absence, the candle gets extinguished.

34. New cars are less polluting than older ones because they are filled with device that changes exhaust gases into CO_2 and H_2O. The device is catalytic converter.

37.